Art Notes, Art

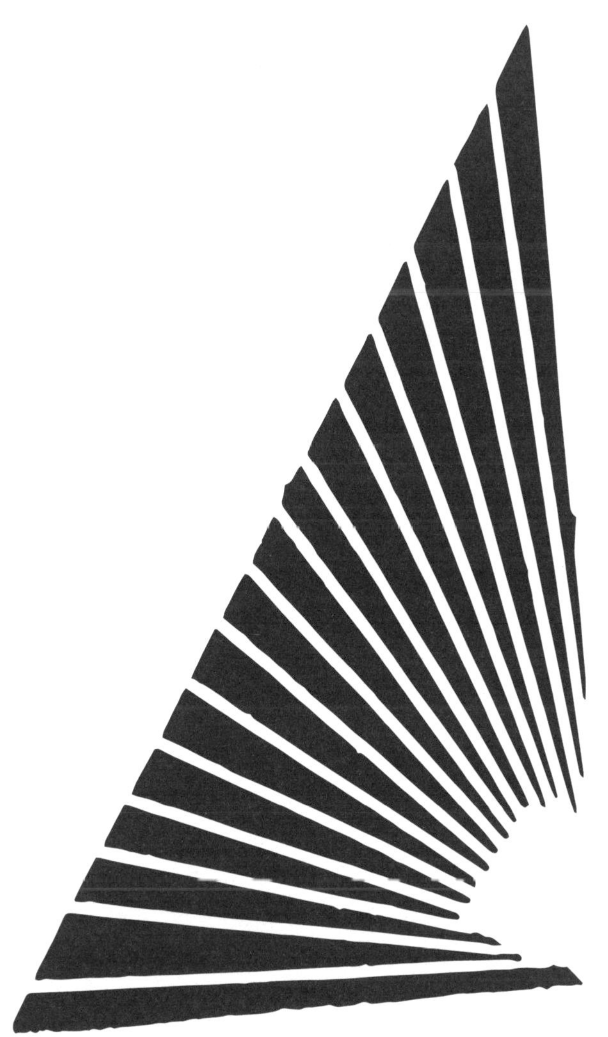

Art Notes, Art

Cynthia Hawkins

Center for Art,
Research and Alliances

CONTENTS

Since I began making art, I have had the desire to discuss art theory and to write down my thoughts about my practice, my ideas, and art more generally. When asked about my work I generally begin at the beginning: in 1972, I entered the art department at Queens College, City University of New York. I still have drawings from 1972; I kept the last figurative painting I completed. Next to me is a notebook, neither the first nor the last, but one that I kept and that contains my ideas and questions about art and painting. The date is October 10, 1973. On the first page are five questions regarding the environment, its effects on painting, and its complexities; the figurative; the environment and abstraction; the minimal; and how those all affect art. The last entry is dated October 14, 1973.

Art Notes, Art (1979–1981) is a continuation of such questions and of my deep engagement with my art practice. My work evolved from figurative and still life content that used gymnastic equipment (Fig. 1). This series of charcoal and pastel drawings developed into geometric abstraction paintings (Fig. 2). My great influences at this time were Johannes Vermeer (1632–1675), Piet Mondrian (1872–1944), and Hans Hoffman (1880–1966). They each played a role in my development: Vermeer with regard to perspective (particularly his floors); Hoffman, color; Mondrian, the evolving drawings and paintings of trees (1910–1912). In particular, Mondrian showed me that the artist could push the natural so hard that it became other than itself.

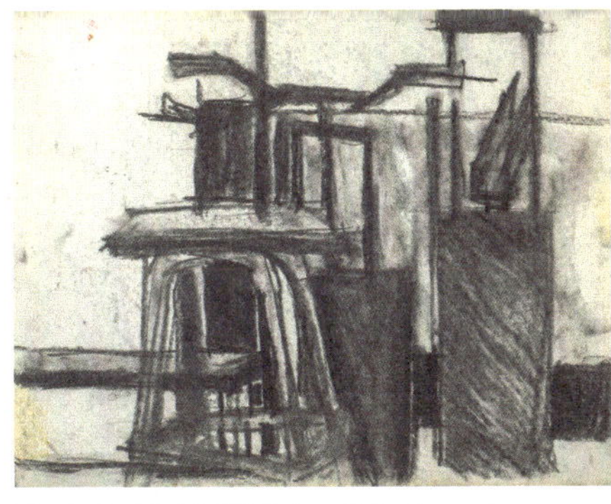

Fig. 1, *Untitled (Still Life)*, c. 1973. Charcoal on paper, 11 × 14 in.

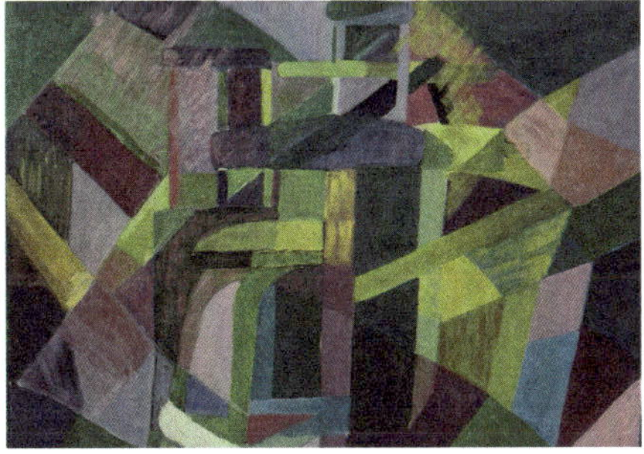

Fig. 2, *Untitled (Geo Abstraction 1)*, c. 1973. Oil on canvas, 24 × 36 in.

I was and continue to be a painter. From 1974 through 1976, I began by drawing a still life with chairs (Fig. 3), then moved to more extensive mark-making (Fig. 4), and then used pastels again (Fig. 5). I created many drawings in which I loosened the pencil work and brought an expressionistic approach to the mark-making. In the summer of 1975, I created several large paintings on paper (Fig. 6). In the fall I returned to pastels, then paintings on canvas (Fig. 7).

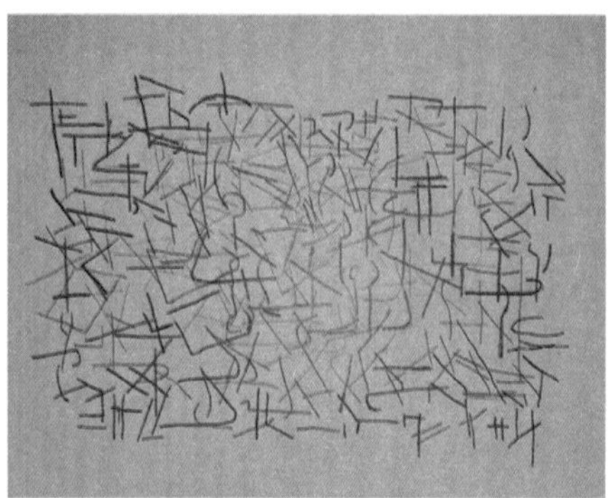

Fig. 3, *Untitled (Still of Chairs)*, 1974. Graphite on paper, 11 × 14 in.

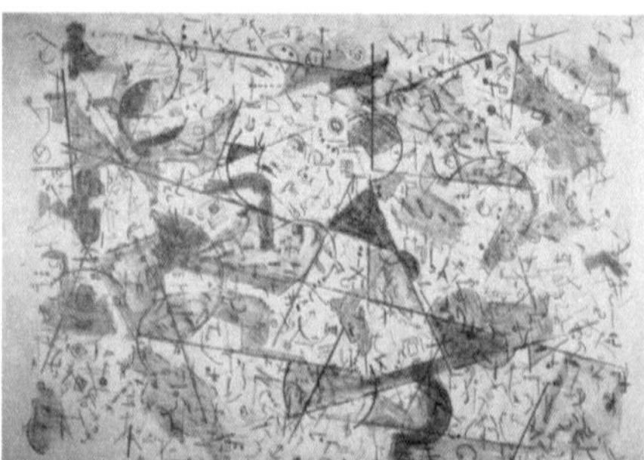

Fig. 4, *Hierog Inner Marks #1*, 1974. Pencil and graphite stick on paper, 20 × 25 in.

This manuscript documents the period between 1979 and 1982 during which I began to make sculpture. My primary material was polyethylene (Fig. 8), followed by wire relief sculptures (Fig. 9), which on one occasion included transistor components (Fig. 10). That was an effort to work through how contemporary industrial components could be useful in another context. By this time, I also began taking artistic influence from my research on black holes and the fourth dimension. I found that visually describing the fourth dimension would require the use of geometry and algebra. Simultaneously, my colleagues developed an interest in the golden ratio, which bore a mathematical relationship to the Fibonacci sequence. I too became interested in using that sequence, as well as sequences of prime numbers, to organize my compositions. (I recently revisited prime numbers for the same reason—to structure composition and color usage.)

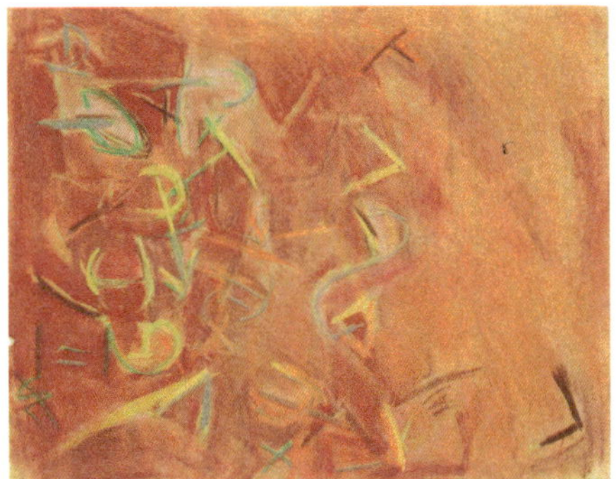

Fig. 5, *Dancing Cubs #1*, 1975. Pastel on paper, 19 ¾ × 25 ½ in.

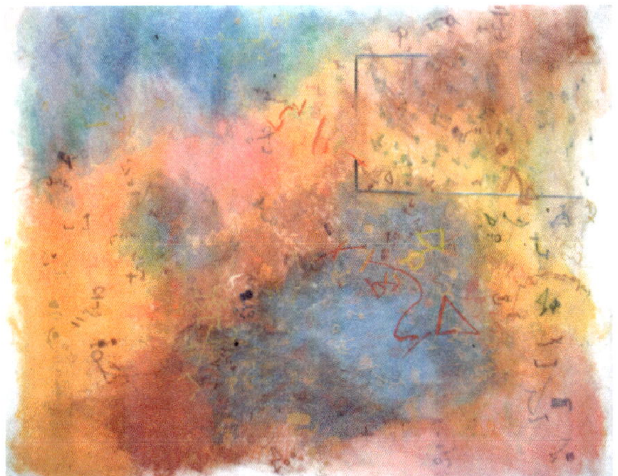

Fig. 6, *Moving Box*, 1975. Oil paint and oil stick on paper, 50 × 60 in.

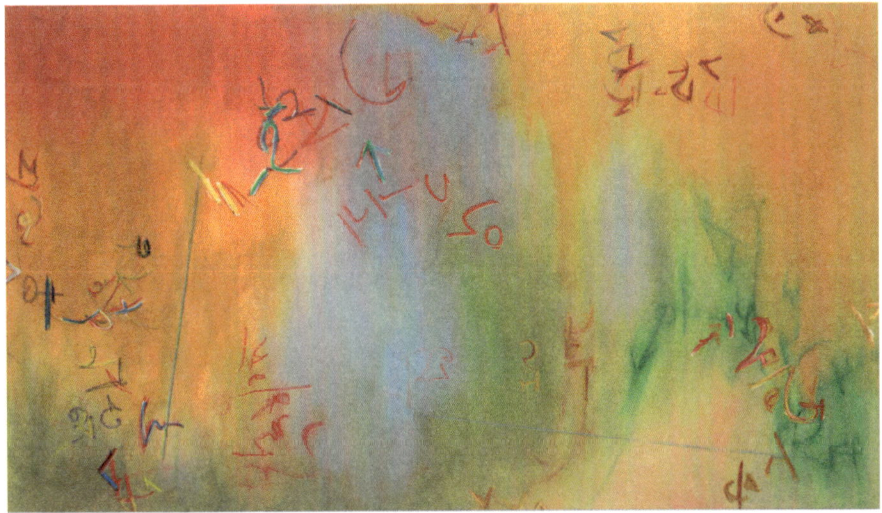

Fig. 7, *Menagerie of Players*, 1975/6. Oil on canvas, 45¾ × 81 in.

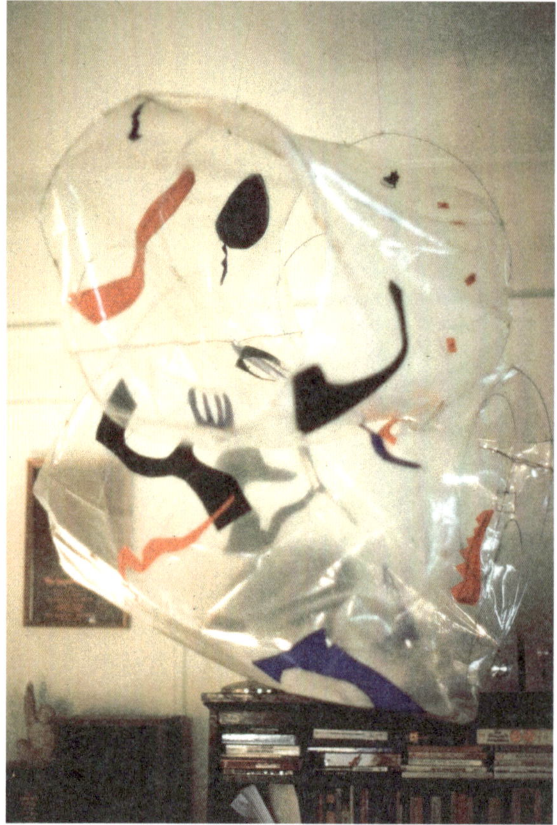

Fig. 8, *Stages*, 1978. Polyethylene and mixed media, dimensions variable.

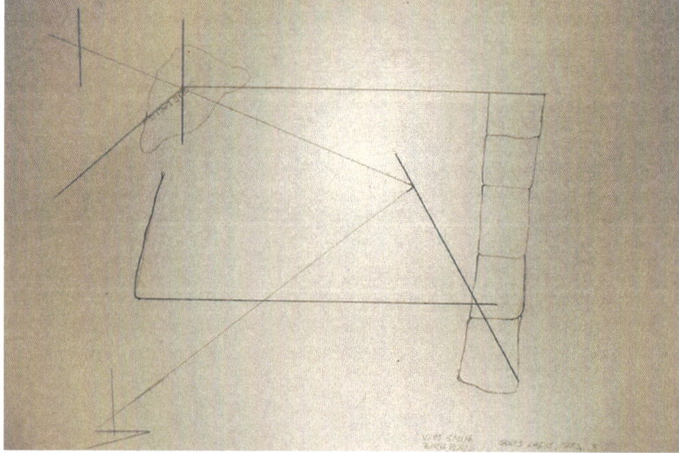

Fig. 9, *Solus Lacus*, 1978. Wire, 20 × 30 in.

Always intending to publish this manuscript, I carried it with me through every move, every life transition. However, the relief sculptures made during this time are no longer extant—on one move, I made the decision to let them go because I was concerned about the artistic integrity of the malleable wire forms supported by Masonite. It only recently occurred to me that this manuscript is an act of recovery, a project to bring into the world that which has been lost. It is fortunate that I retained for my personal archive the slides documenting my work (poor quality as they might be), and I can now share them with you. Through this documentation my trajectory as an artist can be understood not just textually, but visually.

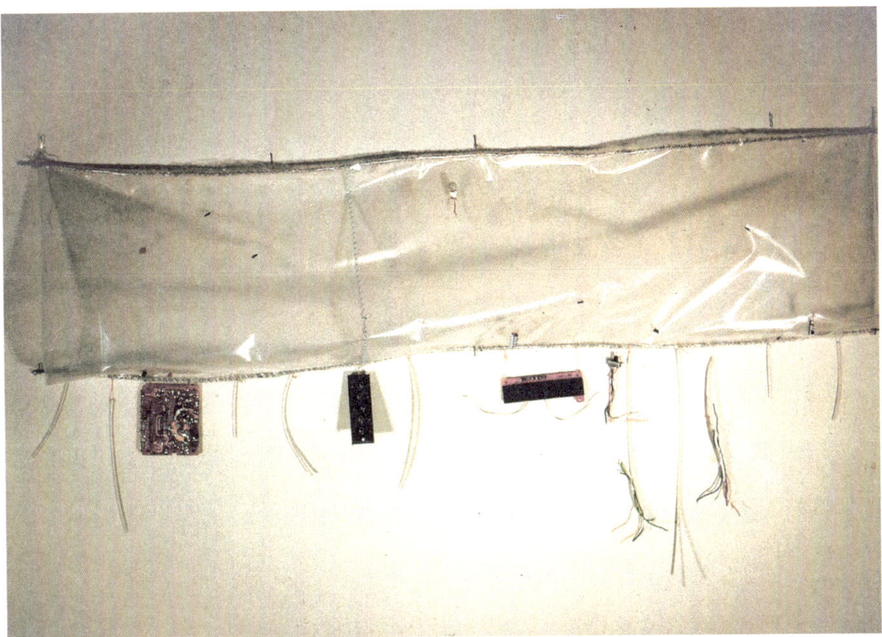

Fig. 10, *Bugs*, 1978. Polyethylene, wire, and transistor parts, 18 × 48 in.

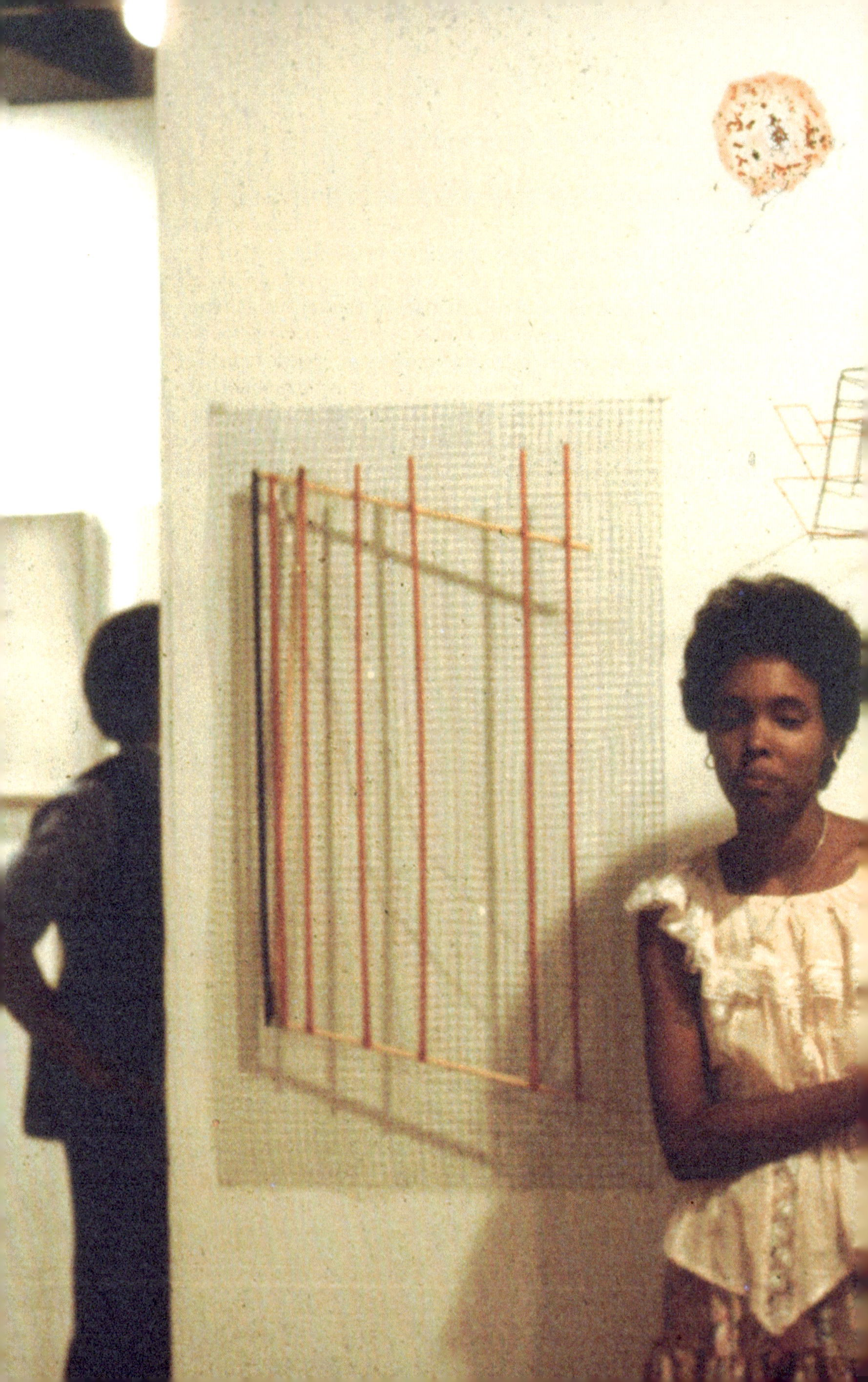

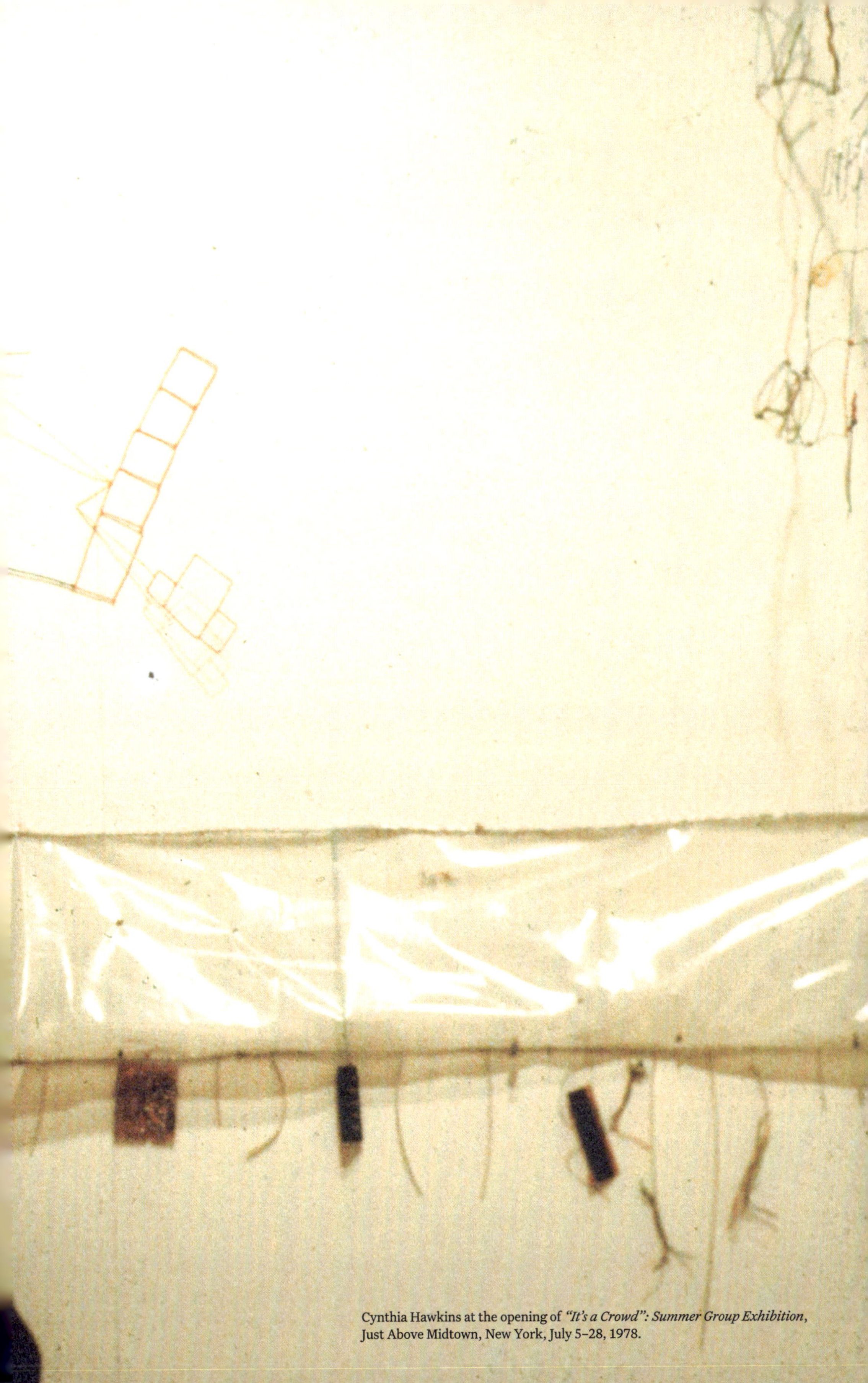

Cynthia Hawkins at the opening of *"It's a Crowd": Summer Group Exhibition*, Just Above Midtown, New York, July 5–28, 1978.

1979

Notes on Bernar Venet[1]

From an article in *Artforum*, January 1979, page 2:
idea of "carry-overs from an older esthetic"[2]

—Rational image (denotative cannot exist without corresponding material support)

"In other words, from what constitutes the proper form for art the debate has now been extended to what constitutes its proper content."[3]

a) What the work is about is completely revealed—stripping off the layering reveals what is. There is no guesswork, since Venet believes that the medium should support but not alter art's content.

[1] Bernar Venet (1941–) is a French painter, sculptor, and early conceptual artist I first became interested in because he was idea-oriented; it wasn't so much about the physical work, but about his process of thinking about it and manifesting it from his intellectual, philosophical position. I also appreciated that he used mathematics as content: some of his early work makes graphical use of mathematical formulas, whether on the canvas or on the page. He was showing around New York in the 1970s and '80s, which is when I first saw his work [Venet moved to New York in 1966].
[2] Jan van der Marck, "Bernar Venet and the Rational Image," *Artforum* 17, no. 5 (January 1979): 2.
[3] Ibid., 14.

"Vernet thus proposes to substitute the non-affective judgment used in science and technology for the subjective or qualitative judgment used in art."[4]

words:

nonsemic
semic

Look for: "The Mathematical Approach in Contemporary Art"[5]

K. T. Fann on Wittgenstein's Conception of Philosophy
Berkeley, 1971, page 41[6]

Postminimalism R. Pincus-Witten[7]

- monosemic
- pansemic
- polysemic[8]

[4] van der Marck, 15.

[5] Max Bill, "The Mathematical Approach to Modern Art," trans. Morton Shand, *Arts & Architecture* 71, no. 8 (August 1954): 20–21.

[6] K. T. Fann, *Wittgenstein's Conception of Philosophy* (Berkeley: University of California Press, 1971).

[7] Robert Pincus-Whitten, *Postminimalism* (New York: Out of London Press, 1978).

[8] In "Bernar Venet and the Rational Image," Jan van der Marck defines these terms through the French cartographer Jacques Bertin: "Bertin calls music and nonfigurative images 'pansemic,' because their meaning is virtually limitless. Verbs and figurative images, on the other hand, may invite different interpretations, but their limited meaning make them 'polysemic'. . . Only mathematics and the graphic image, according to Bertin, qualify as 'monosemic.'" van der Marck, 9fn1. In 2019, I completed my PhD dissertation—titled "African American Agency and the Art Object, 1868–1917"—at SUNY Buffalo. In the process, I encountered Iain D. Thomson's book *Heidegger, Art, and Postmodernity*, and came to a new understanding of polysemy. I wrote: "an artist, painter or musician may create a variety of constructed forms from wood, or a series of notes. In other words, there is no one correct art form to be yielded from the materials at hand. Therefore, polysemy is that which asks each one to envision the possibilities or alternatives to normative pre-existing assumed forms or directive." Cynthia Hawkins, "African American Agency and the Art Object, 1868–1917" (PhD diss., University of Buffalo, New York, 2019), 58.

a) See page 17.

Content

b) Subject matter, as in a book;

c) Meaning or significance.

Rational

c) Based upon reason, logical.

Use of sequences such as linear patterns—i.e., prime numbers.

Linear pattern—does read as a time sequence.

If each unit represents a segment of time, then what occurs in each segment is different, particularly in placement.

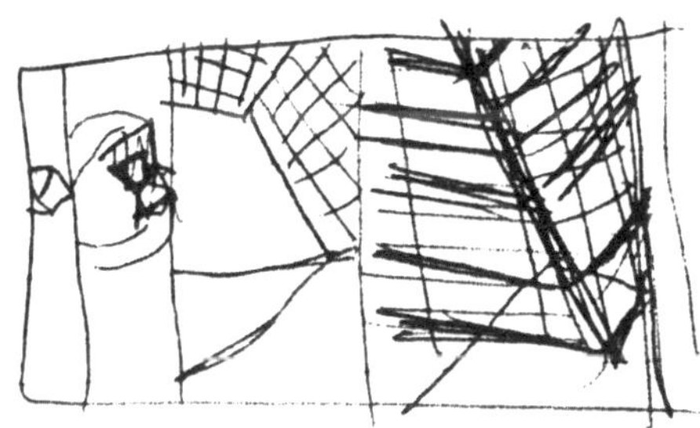

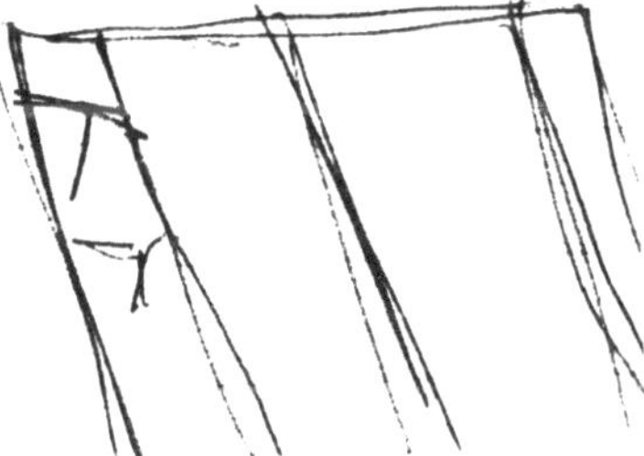

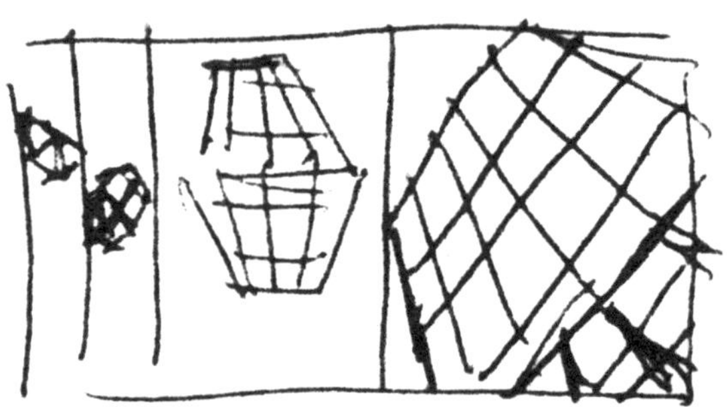

Linear-time sequence and using the line differently to manifest the positions of the object

1) Orbit, which type of orbit?
Circular
Elliptical

Orbit is affected by the curvature of time—

2) Flat time is a box or cube.

3) Learn to draw a fourth-dimensional cube
circle.

Content: orbital movement of a body—the effect the body has on the fabric of space.

b) The vertical demarcations have to do with time intervals and where the body is within a specific interval.

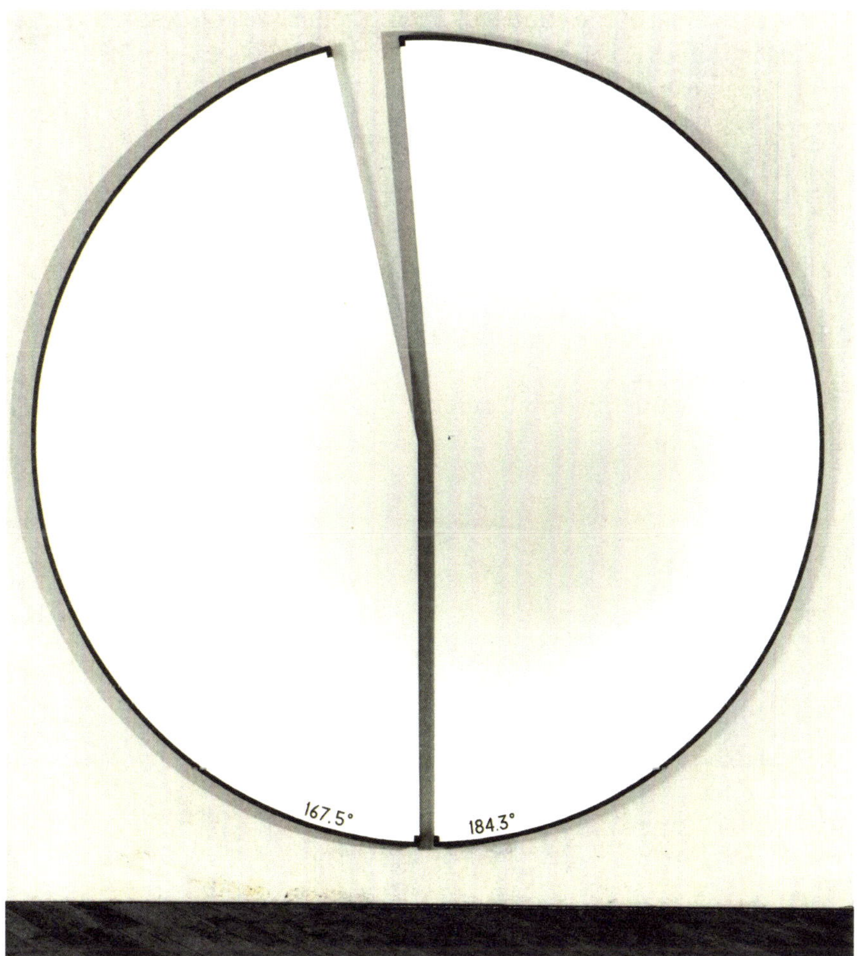

BERNAR VENET, *Position of Two Arcs of 167.5° and 184.3°*, 1978. Acrylic on canvas, 8 ft diameter.

Notes on Pages 19 & 20

The first movement through linear time (sequence on black paper) used red linear demarcations corresponding to the Fibonacci number series.

Fragmented pieces of mesh in the smaller time frame—

It is a reversal of the effective vision. Seen from a distance, the illusory effect is the body moving in the original arc, the bent or foreshortened arc of a circle.

2) Will do another using the white as a marker for a linear sequence—

I guess I did it backward because the smaller frames have smaller areas. So instead of making small rectilinear forms that fragment as they get bigger . . .

*Must try again the prime number linear series.

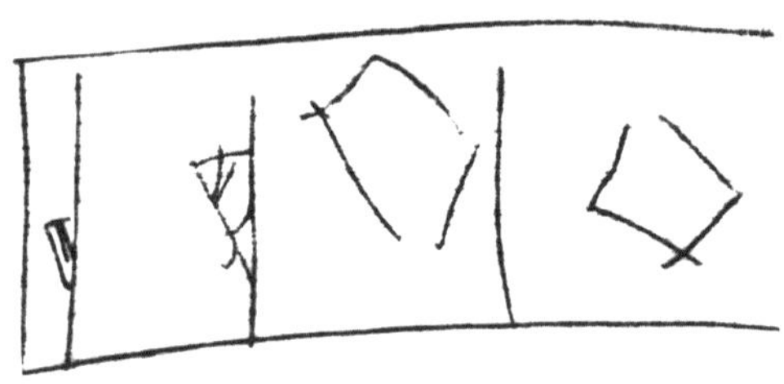

The syntactical structure of the work:

Words such as form, content, and intent take on new or different meanings according to the syntactical arrangement or structure of the work.[9]

Currently the usage of time in my work is very classical, uninterpreted, and one-dimensional (must read again *Einstein's Universe*).[10]

This syntactical usage is why we can come up with new compound words like monosemic and pansemic.[11]

[9] A syntax comprised not of words and phrases, but of visual elements such as line and color.

[10] Nigel Calder, *Einstein's Universe* (New York: Viking Press, 1979).

[11] Ibid., 14.

In the black pieces is the classical usage of linear time, moving from left to right vertically. Then there is the movement of the body across the field (looking through a lens). Simultaneously, there is the body's static rotation on a longer path that takes it across our field of vision.[12]

*Since the field is oriented toward a lens, use the circle or oval instead of using the rectangular shape of the field.

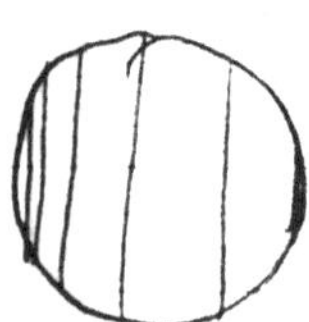

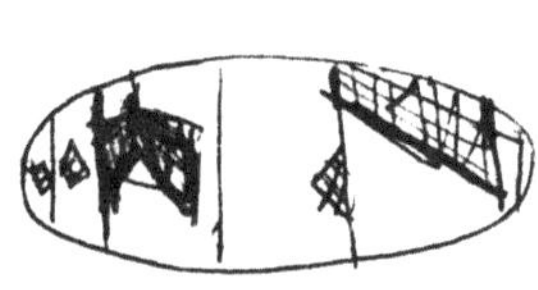

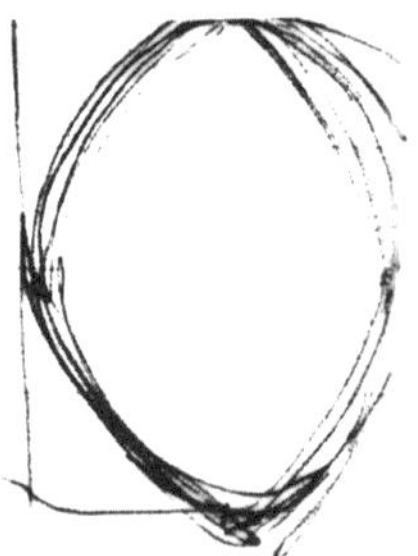

[12] Without a reference point, a rotating or otherwise moving object may appear static.

Thought! Alternate white & black as background; only the wall is included as background.

Make 3 or 4 boxes (drawing 2D or 3D).

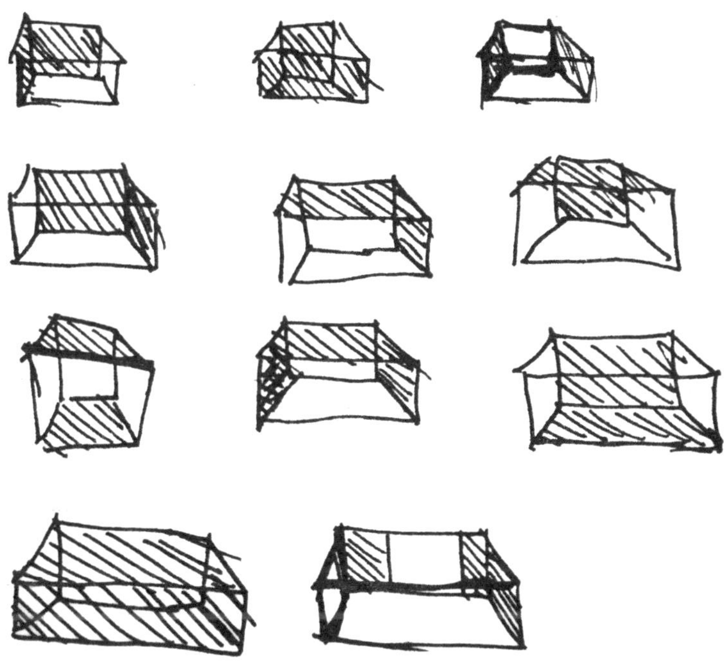

Black and white

Sometimes the urge to make art is so strong I want to scream to get rid of it.
But I do not.
I try to channel it into work . . . sometimes it makes me do nothing.

This is not a fantasy, it is real.
I can see that this is not a fantasy . . .

I must make art.

I am thinking about the artwork. I am a little worried about it becoming too painterly.

Now, this means that—maybe I'm getting slightly mixed up.

I must, I guess, reaffirm my ideas as to what art is, or rather what kind of art I am involved in.
"The idea is paramount."
The idea is more important than anything else.

Bending lines like drawing . . .
so it can be understood from this little sketch.

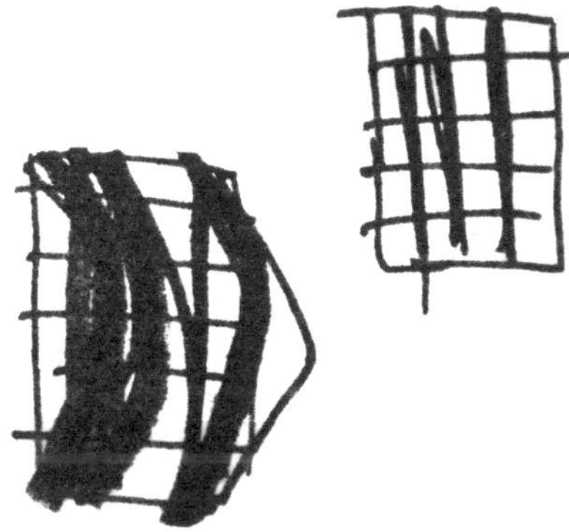

"Where mesh pieces come off the Masonite."

Horizo-lines

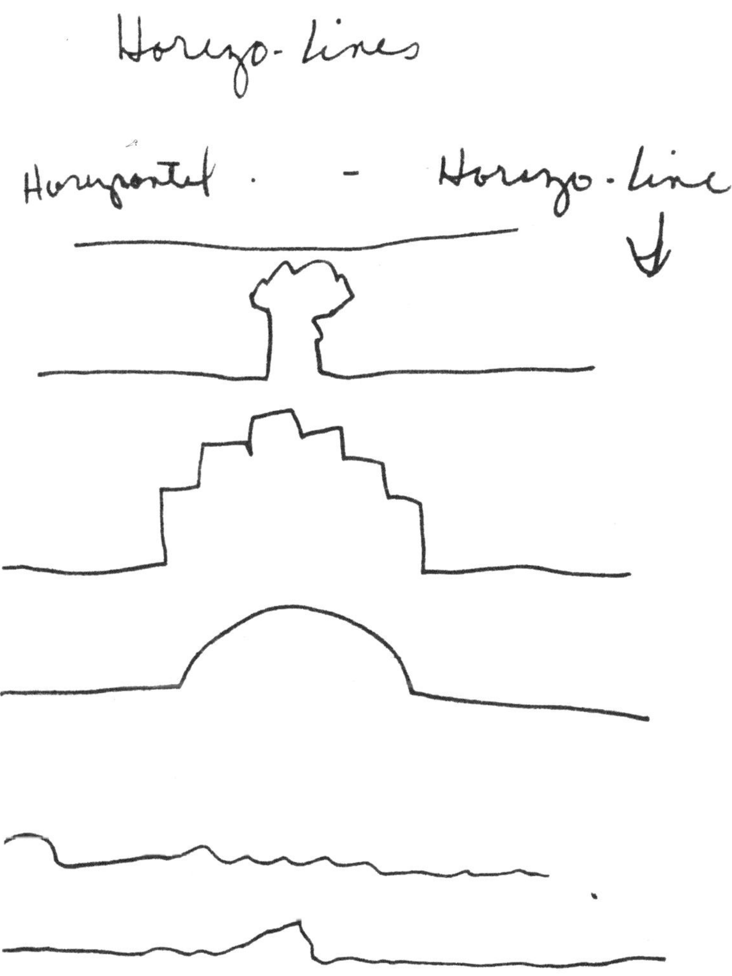

"Horizontal–Horizon-line."

The idea is make a series
of drawings for

HORIZO-LINE -

Variegated plane (planet; moving bodies) on different paper arrangements.

On Masonite place a grid or a linear sequence, and—as mentioned on page 27—a piece of mesh with painted stripes. Bend it in various shapes to illustrate curved space to some degree or another—

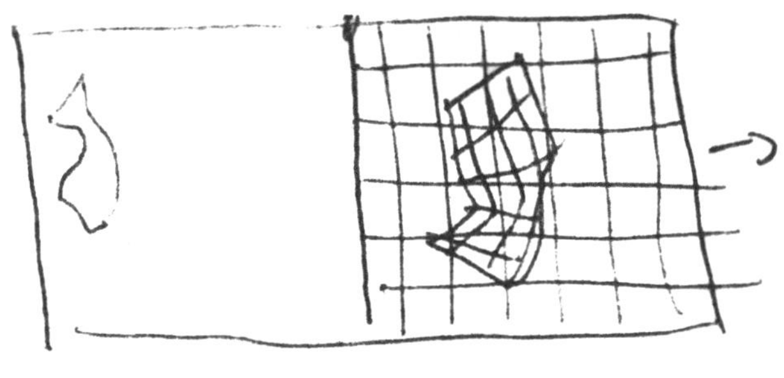

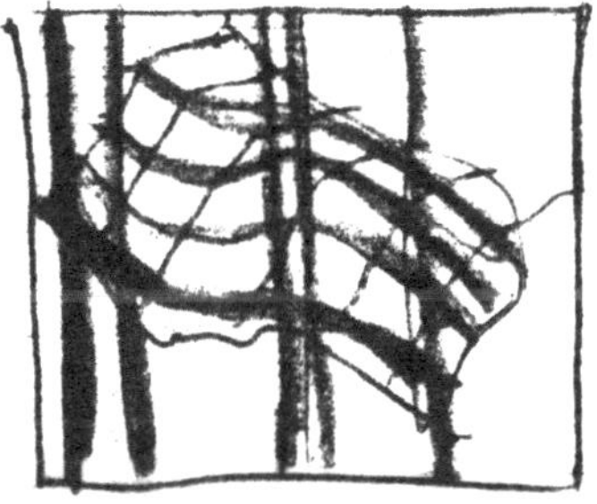

"Reversing the lines on the paper so that the lines seem distorted and the mesh seems straight (5/79)."

First, I should say I have had thoughts about page 30.
I am going to make the body or what I feel like calling the fish, the exact same.[13]
The fish on the plane is non-linear and the linear part—FLAT—vertical
horizontal
primary (background)
Fibonacci sequence

[13] I got tired of repeating the word "body" and briefly replaced it with "fish."

I can remember what I may have mentioned before—using the curved lines—

What I recall is the curving of the lines of the proposed body, but not necessarily the space. With this other proposal on pages 30 and 32, I will use the curved space lines also.

I may eliminate the white ground—it's kind of sterile.

The meeting is here tonight—I am trying to think about what I am going to say.[14]

1) I want to talk about the white ground on the pieces in the room.

2) About the pieces being too painterly.

3) Maybe I am using too much extra paper.

4) How do people feel about the work in general—

[14] I was part of a group called Ten Women. We were all artists and would meet to discuss our work.

Yesterday was Monday, June 4th, 1979.

I was at a seminar of art critics.[15]
I found out some very interesting things about being an art critic.
While artists make no money, critics from magazines can make 50 dollars a month.
In any case, the two critics were Barbara Cavaliere of *Arts Magazine* and Margie Bettes of *Art News*.

[15] Linda Goode Bryant invited the critics Barbara Cavaliere and Margie Bettes to speak at Just Above Midtown as part of "The Business of Being an Artist" sessions, which were aimed at artists' professional development. In this seminar, Cavaliere spoke specifically about what she did as a critic and what kind of living a critic made. I remember clearly that she mentioned how little money they were paid for reviews.

Must rework the first black piece.

The diagonal lines can be worked into the primary Fibonacci linear series but put on a diagonal. I like how the single large piece of mesh is placed and warped.

This black one looks very beautiful to me. In a lyrical way, it speaks to me of regularity and irregularity, which relates to life. Is the organic regular or irregular? Chemically it is regular, but in those instances where something violently new is added by chance, those new elements can be considered irregular.

I want to add that I have found a way to deal with the nine-room occurrence.

That is to build nine boxes 3 × 3 × 3 feet or 2 × 3 × 3 feet. The outside would be white, and the demarcations would be black. There would be three boxes to a wall, each wall representing a floor.

1) They would be made from ¼-inch plywood or pine

2) And the wood would be painted matte white on the outside and matte black on the inside

I made a cardboard prototype to gauge the size of one box. Decided on 16 × 24 × 8 for each. The material is knotty pine or Masonite—I prefer knotty pine of ¼-inch width. Now, however, the problem is whether the individual boxes should stand vertically or horizontally.

The vertical gives the sense of a building (architecture) and the horizontal the sense of a room or stage. I think the horizontal is more comfortable for me. There definitely appears to be a psychology to the box being horizontal or vertical. While thinking these things I think of the chauvinists.[16]

[16] At the time, artists and theorists were assigning gender to everything—horizontal was construed as feminine and vertical as masculine.

I discussed the vertical versus the horizontal with Brenda Kristal.[17] She said that the horizontal is synonymous with rooms, or rather the shape of a room; also, that it would be more challenging to have the boxes vertical rather than horizontal, which I agree with. The horizontal seems to be a restful position and nine horizontals would put one to sleep. I am apprehensive about the vertical, but I'll do it that way regardless. I also think it might have something to do with personality as well as conditions. How we relate to the horizontal shape is 90 percent conditioning.

However, I just thought of Jessica[18]—and all the spirituality of the golden mean.[19] I wonder if all of the calming things Jessica spoke of are really true. Can their effect be measured? In any case, the viewer as well as myself both need to be jolted into action, intellectually and visually.

[17] Brenda Kristal was my friend in the art department at Queens College and in the women artists' group we were part of. Her medium was glass sculpture—her family owned a glass business in SoHo. Brenda stopped working on art in the early 1980s. At the time, I remember visiting her near Columbus Avenue and 74th Street, but she had discontinued her art practice.

[18] Jessica Hart is a New England-based artist and former freelance textile designer. She was briefly part of the Ten Women artists' group, during which time she was also involved in painting.

[19] This refers to the golden ratio of mathematics and visual art, as opposed to the philosophical golden mean (the desired middle between excess and deprivation).

Must think of outdoor project in the Wall Street area.

8/21/79
I did decide on something, a game called *Primarily Art*. I sent the design to Linda[20] before Steven and I left for Montreal.[21]

It's a numeric grid on a box. Holes are cut into the box where a prime number falls. You try to get the red and yellow chips into the holes.

Two people should play at a time. When you miss the hole, you create a drawing using the random arrangement of the red and yellow chips on the surface.

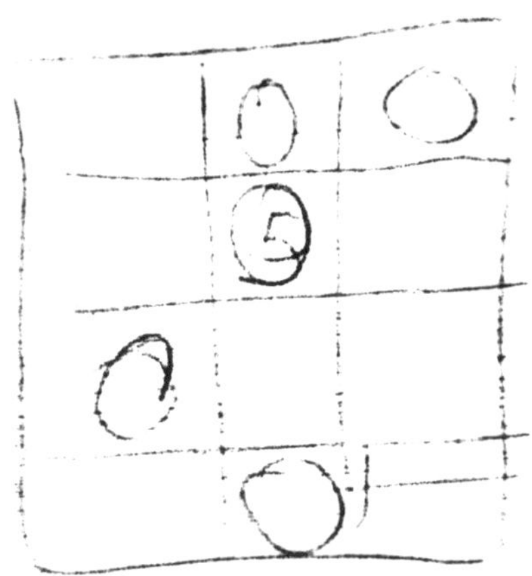

[20] Linda Goode Bryant (1949–) is a former gallerist based in New York, a farmer, and filmmaker. I first met her by happenstance in the spring of 1978 during one of my regular Saturday afternoon visits to see gallery exhibitions on 57th Street. I walked into Just Above Midtown (JAM), which was located at 50 W. 57th Street, and saw her sitting at the desk. I had never met a Black woman who owned a gallery before. I introduced myself, eventually asked if I could show there. David Hammons was there that day—he nodded, yes. In July 1978, my work was included in the summer group exhibition "*It's a Crowd.*" I continued to go to JAM all the time, and in the summer of 1980, the gallery moved downtown to Franklin Street [178–80 Franklin Street]. I had my first solo show there the next year.

[21] Steven Chaiken was my partner at the time (we were married for something like seven years). He was an aspiring actor when we met—he had gotten a degree in theater from Stony Brook—and later decided to become a lawyer.

I took the white boundary off a piece of white paper. I still have questions about it (it leaves me cold).

However, I did three more black pieces. As yet there are no bodies on them, but the drawing part on two of them is, I think, beautiful. One is called *Time Like* and the other (horizontal) is *Space Like*.

I am searching for a definition of formalism. I understand what it is in an intuitive way.

I dealt with it specifically when I was making paintings. When formalism was brought up in a meeting, others who have been making paintings and sculpture said they had talked about it but didn't really understand it or could not give a definition. My interest was that not all artwork uses that method—and as Irene Wheeler suggested, the meaning of formalism changes with the type of work one does.[22] As a method, formalism has boundaries.

Reading *Art on the Edge* by Harold Rosenburg leads to thoughts about formalism.[23]

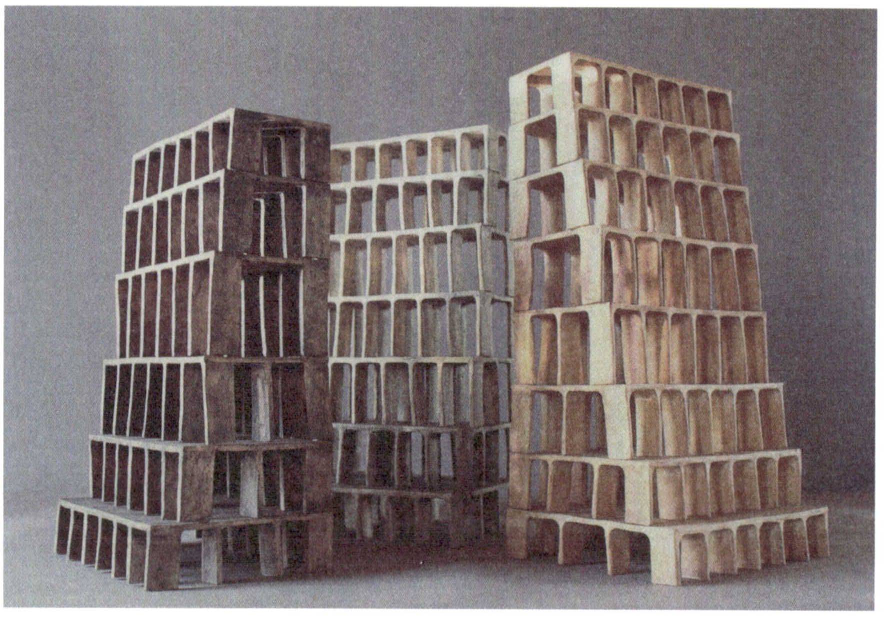

IRENE WHEELER, *Beirut*, 1980. Oxidized clay.

[22] Irene Wheeler (1917–2003) was a ceramic sculptor and my dear friend and mentor. I met Irene at Queens College when I was in my twenties and she in her fifties. She introduced me to artists such as Norman Lewis, Romare Bearden, and Ernie Crichlow, who were all co-founders of Cinque Gallery in New York, where I had a solo show in 1989 [*New Works: The Currency of Meaning*]. I knew her as a charming and generous person. She bought one of my paintings, and I later found out that she had donated it to The Studio Museum [*Currency in Meaning #11*, 1989, oil on canvas, 77⅜ × 57⅜ × 2½ in.].
[23] Harold Rosenberg, *Art on the Edge: Creators and Situations* (Chicago: University of Chicago Press, 1975).

One—Formalism is a consideration of parts or elements, i.e., the skeleton of painting and sculpture.

Two—Formalism is a method of considering an art object and its development.

Three—To use the formalist method, one must be "objet d'art" oriented.[24]

[24] In retrospect, this is not accurate. I was confusing the ornamental "objet d'art" with the formalist idea of analyzing art for its own sake. A formalist practice centers color, line, form, and texture, and is not invested in narrative or function. Formalism seeks its own intelligibility; it is separate from the things of life.

Notes by myself found in books on Constructivism:

It is the place between painting and sculpture. It is not sculpture in the least traditional manner—except by its own nature in the world. It is not painting in any traditional manner except that some kind of paint may be applied to some surface. From there on, there is no similarity.
Its aim is to defy natural and/or visual boundaries.

Constructivism, by my definition, says you can no longer be one or the other, but that both must work towards the unification of art. Constructivism works through a total experience; my work comes about through math, science, reading. The desire is to lift or rather to expand what I call the tunnel vision of the art community and the society.

More notes on formalism:

"Formalistic theories are linked to a new interest in the course of the eighteenth century, from which time the unconscious aesthetic impulse has gradually emerged to awareness as a deliberately cultivated value."[25]

[25] Harold Osborne, *Aesthetics and Art Theory: An Historical Introduction* (New York: E. P. Dutton, 1970), 306–307.

I finally managed to fix the two body pieces. There are two completed. One body is on a white background and the (almost) identical body is on black. The white body is marked with vertical red tape corresponding to the Fibonacci lines and the black body is marked with horizontal tape in the same fashion. The horizontal works better because its appearance is not as rigid, whereas the vertical lines on the paper and on the mesh echo each other too much. The vertical lines are now connected to the body set on a diagonal. The body on the horizontal is also set on a diagonal. The piece makes more sense now. I hope it is apparent—the use of two same or similar bodies in one piece.

In addition, the shadows cast by the mesh bodies, when they appear on the paper, bring to mind the use of more organic lines. For this I would get some contact paper (in red) to cut out the wavy lines. And I would use it to accentuate some lines cast in the shadows.

I think I should log that I will be in three group shows this year:

1) Emily Lowe Gallery in Hempstead, Long Island.[26]

2) A traveling exhibition at Jamaica Arts Center[27]—then it will be moving to the Bronx Museum.

3) The opening group show at Just Above Midtown's new location on Franklin Street.[28]

Now I must look back to see where I was headed in the artwork before work starts again in September and I start going to sleep at eleven thirty (which doesn't interfere with my work at all, but for some reason I'm using it as an excuse).

[26] Financed in 1951 by Miami philanthropists Joe and Emily Lowe, this gallery is now part of the Hofstra University Museum of Art.
[27] The Jamaica Center for Arts and Learning was founded in 1972 in Jamaica, Queens, New York.
[28] Just Above Midtown was founded by Linda Goode Bryant in 1974 and closed in 1986. For more information, see Linda Goode Bryant, Thomas J. Lax, and Lilia Rocio Taboada, eds., *Just Above Midtown: Changing Spaces* (New York: The Museum of Modern Art/The Studio Museum in Harlem, 2022).

My new pieces will work off the telescopic view of bodies in space.

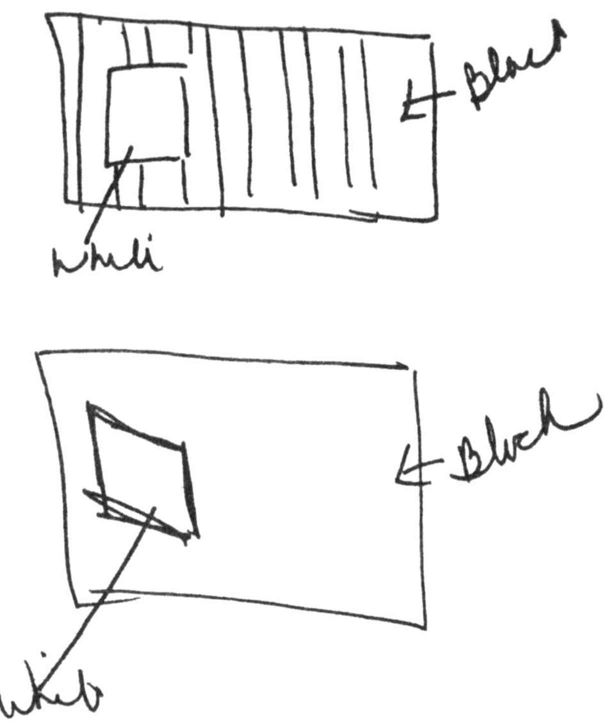

Arrows indicate black and white sections.

The diagonally placed white paper will enhance the two different sightings.

The white, of course, is what is seen through the telescope; and the black, what may really be.

The window

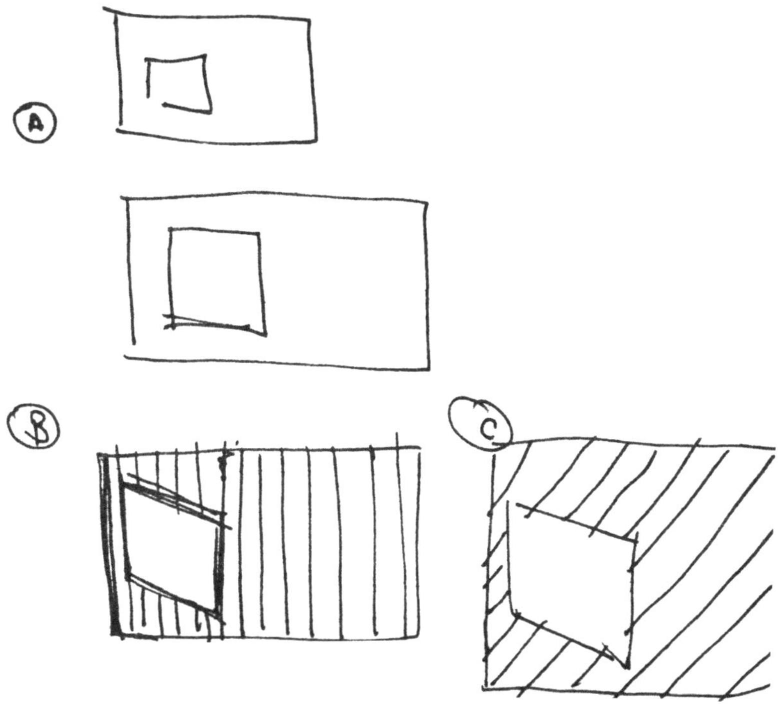

Verticals set at varying intervals (must find or make another rational sequence).

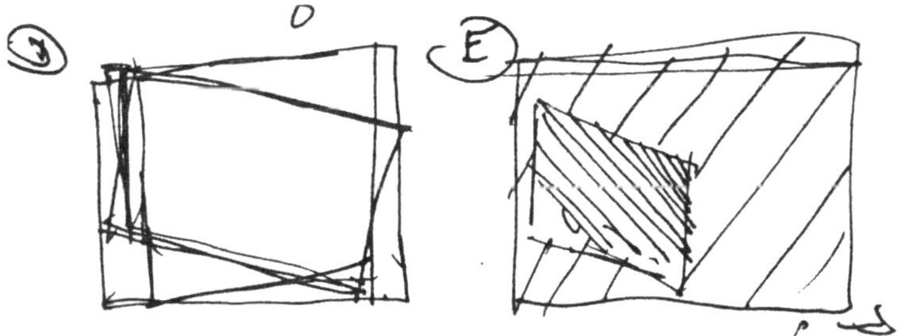

B through E are more visually interesting. They may be reminiscent of some flags, but that is not their function. The mesh may be placed on both black and white or on only one color.

F—mesh on both white and black
G—only on black
H—only on white
I—only on white

Maybe I better introduce yellow.

I tried describing an organic line on the *Bent 4*, *5*, and *6*—but it no longer thrills me.

A) Boxes
B) Corner installation
C) Windows—*Vue Deux Fois*

Suddenly it seems like summer or near summer, I don't know. The feeling must come from some summer past. Some summer probably before Steven. The creativity one feels when making a piece is not always apparent. When certain unnamed things come together it becomes apparent. I think the weather this time tipped the scales toward realization.

The piece I am about to do, which I have partly completed, lets me know it is aptly named: *Twice Seen*, or in French, as it shall be titled, *Vue Deux Fois*. It is not often a person can intellectually perceive and identify and know—at the bringing together of paper, tape, and mesh—that it is right.

I really did need this to be so with *Vue Deux Fois* because the *Bent 4*, *5*, and *6*, are the metamorphosing of three other pieces: *Bent Bodies 1*, *2*, and *3*. Even now the *Bent Bodies 4*, *5*, and *6* are satisfactory, but not satisfying in my heart. It is rather disheartening. But one must have these disappointments so one can recognize the true work of art. *Vue Deux Fois* puts my mind at peace. There is no need to worry about the work at this moment.

It would have been really nice if I hadn't run out of red tape!

The first group show opens Nov. 14. I found out we have to write a statement for the catalogue. I wrote two—I feel both are inadequate.

This is what Linda Bryant sent to Emily Lowe:

> My work is about the utilization of ideas. Through the use of simple, everyday material—materials not special. The work becomes art—which is then called special.
>
> My work is somewhere between painting and sculpture. I am able to take from both forms—therefore, the work has the widest possible historic references available to it—by not being distinctly of either form.
>
> The idea is of most importance. My work comes from my life experiences and from factual information from many areas—mainly science and philosophy.

Maybe I should call Linda and tell her she can edit it as she sees fit. I don't feel it is adequate. Maybe I should call Irene Wheeler and read it to her.

I did call Irene. We decided to take out the sentence that mentions the word "special."

Today, 11/6, Jessie[29] and Brenda came over to see the pieces before I take them to Linda's apartment. I got good, rather excellent reviews from both of them. I also only received ten invitations.

P.S. I am very excited now. It's really going to happen!

[29] Jessie may refer to a physical therapist who was Irene Wheeler's friend.

There was a small catalogue made to go along with the show. In it, Linda wrote, “Hawkins playfully challenges . . . ” I think “playfully” is the wrong word.

Have been working on *Vue Deux Fois*. It's been in my head for a few weeks now. Again, the push was the deadline—the group is coming here Monday.

First, I realized how the lines of the smaller white part were drawn wrong. It wouldn't have appeared wrong to anyone else, but they were wrong to me.
Second, I made a few parallelograms and used vertical and horizontal lines. When put on the approx. 45° of some line, the verticals and horizontals become diagonals, that's good.
Third, since I didn't have enough red tape, I found the blue and used it for the larger verticals moving across the black outer field.

Then I tried replacing the white field area and only using white horizontal lines on a plain black field, and then using the Fibonacci line (which I did differently this time) and the primary number line with yellow and blue respectively.
I haven't worked on the bodies yet. But so far, I am satisfied—more ideas coming up for the possible variations.
I just remembered that I can only use the black field either plain or with vertical mesh . . .
Most of the variegated action must take place on the smaller closed field areas.

The smaller areas, which are white and lined, will be referred to as the closed fields. The closed fields have quite a few possibilities. They can also be used to gauge distance. See diagram below.

Even though the closed field already represents a closer view, the body on the open field must be smaller and the body on the closed field larger. I must see how it will work; might have to reverse this.

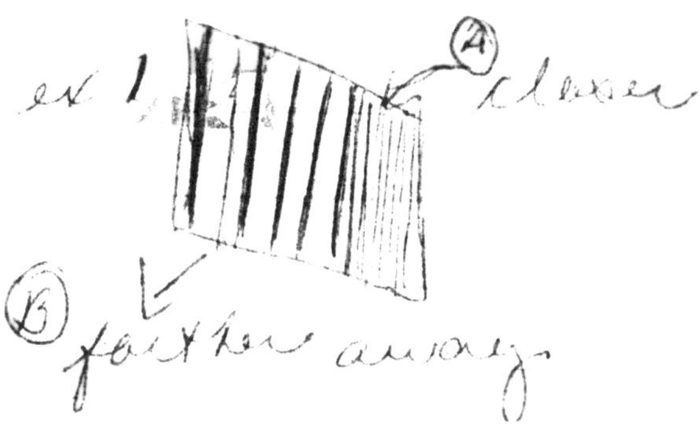

Arrows mark where the verticals are A) closer together and B) farther away.

The meeting is here tonight.

I'm trying to think of things to say as an introduction.

a) Show slides—what they looked like then and now.

b) Studio, new pieces.

After-meeting notes:

1) Maybe make closed field pieces.
Make a bigger piece, discuss with self the purpose of making a bigger piece.
Use bigger or smaller mesh—
I wonder which mesh parts of the pieces seem integrated enough.

The group likes this direction.

Brenda says I'm dealing with more sculptural space than before.

Maybe it is a series—they are called *Vue Deux Fois*.

Jessie asked if I thought of these pieces as a series. No, I don't.

I am now reading *The Lives of a Cell* by Lewis Thomas.[30]

I have realized while reading these very good and comforting essays that the problem with art is that there is no touching, no open discourse, no hashing out ideas. There is no place for discourse, no center where people/artists can talk together. I believe the problem is not that there are too many artists, because there are too many of everybody; the problem is not jealousy, or fear of being ripped off, because that is also in every place and profession. If there is any reason, it is that too many artists believe their own myths. I think probably many scientists believe their myth, too. However, their myth is one of collaboration, one of discussion; even though some, let's say 50% of the research, may go on in isolation. Whereas the artist works in isolation and continues so.

Artists believe in the myth that only through extraordinary effort can artists group themselves for the purpose of discourse, remain a group for at the very most two years. The position of the artist is supported by the gallery and museum system. There are too many artists wanting not to be rich, but just to have their names known. To try and consolidate as professionals (in or out of the university system). I must mention that I am part of a group of women that meets to discuss our work and ideas. But meeting every two or three weeks is not enough. There is not enough variety in the discussion because not everyone is interested in the aesthetic or philosophical fields. In my work I want to try to incorporate everything I learn. I am influenced by everything I read. There is much to coalesce. I, myself, as an artist, want more in the way of discourse. For this reason, I'm almost sure I want to study philosophy.

[30] Lewis Thomas, *The Lives of a Cell: Notes of a Biology Watcher* (New York: Viking Press, 1974).

I think I'd like to create/develop/make a small art journal. Maybe call it *Artverb* or *Artwrite* or *Writing About Art—WAA*. I like *Artwrite* or *Artverb*.
I would print it three to four times a year, quarterly (I think that's four times).

Anyway, I could have in it three major articles and some shorter writings.
I could get some artists to write about art or some ideas they are thinking or some long-established dictums. Opinions also.

It would be cheap/inexpensive; I would have it Xerox- or offset-printed. Subscription would be about ten dollars a year. That's very cheap, and I'm not doing it for the money, anyway.

In response to Hal Foster's article "A Tournament of Rose's"[31]:

I agree with Mr. Foster's conclusion that serious ambition is lacking. For me this statement includes most painters today. There are many people painting in ways they think are different. Painting needs an internal life, not just a facial. I have also seen artists assume a type or style of painting without a synthesis that makes the work one's own.

As far as I'm concerned, I never thought painting lacked humanism. Humans make paintings; therefore, it cannot be anything else.

[31] Hal Foster, "A Tournament of Rose's," *Artforum* 18, no. 3 (November 1979): 62–67.

However, in conceptual and performance art, there can be an over-dependence on machines, materials, and technique. These two problems are the extremes of one half or another. But this extreme dependency has the same root cause as external, face-lifting approaches to painting. I think we are probably after the same thing: to give art in general something more, something that really differentiates it from earlier work, so we don't feel like we're relying on the past but innovating for the future.

Generally, I think many artists have become weighed down by the history of art instead of using it to uplift our world, our work, our art. History provides examples of what can be achieved through both analysis and an internal synthesis of art and technology.

All in all, Hal Foster's article was very good, very good indeed.

I have read again *The Courage to Create*.[32]

Again, it is a fascinating book.

This time I am taking away the idea of boundaries.

[32] Rollo May, *The Courage to Create* (New York: Bantam Books, 1976).

It’s about to be accepted into verse.

1980

I went to the Whitney Museum. There was a show of David Smith's drawings.[33] A few were really interesting. What drew my attention is the fervor that comes across in the drawings. The energy, vitality of David Smith's creativity.

The most intriguing aspect of these particular drawings was the use of spray paint. The spray painting of the objects and ground made the objects integral, lighthearted, free-floating—as bodies moving serenely in space.

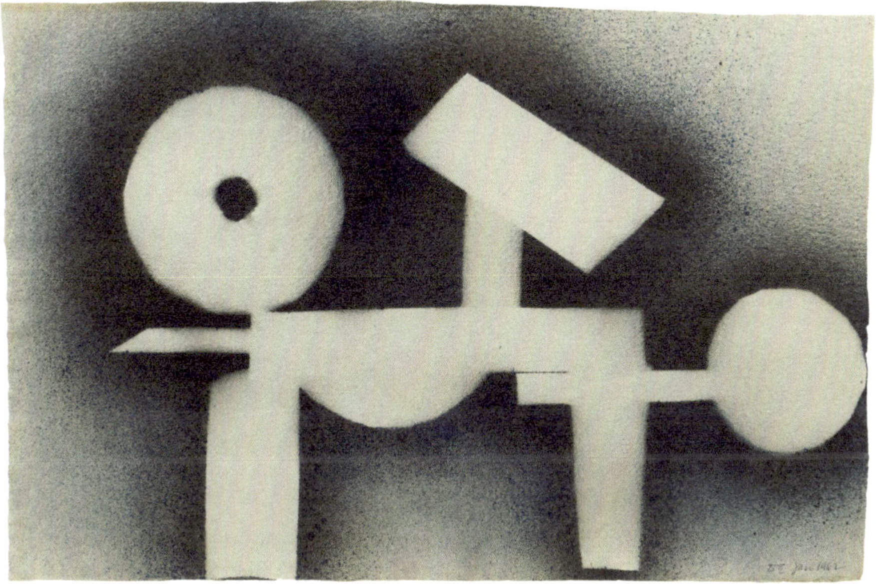

DAVID SMITH, *Untitled*, 1962. Spray enamel on paper, 13 × 20 in (33 × 50.8 cm).

[33] *David Smith: The Drawings*, Whitney Museum, New York, December 4, 1979 to February 24, 1980.
David Smith (1906–1965) was an American sculptor and painter. I responded to his three-dimensional work, but found especially interesting his drawings, which are very graphical.

I also saw Cynthia Gallagher's work at Borgenicht Gallery.[34] I had seen at least one of them previously—the one that has a lot of red in it.

I also liked the painting by Louisa Chase.[35] She used to make boxed sculptures—very small boxes with little things in them, like diagrams. Now she makes paintings that are personal, iconographic, and symbolic.

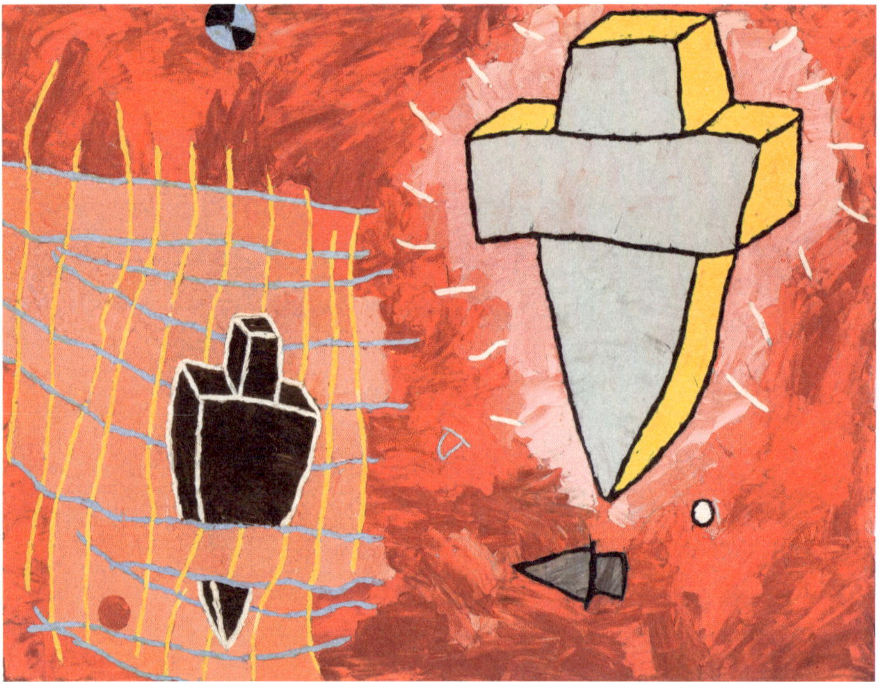

LOUISA CHASE, *Untitled*, c. 1979. Oil and wax on canvas, 36¼ × 49½ in.

[34] *On Paper* (group exhibition), Grace Borgenicht Gallery, New York, 1980.
Cynthia Gallagher (1951–) is an American artist who makes very energetic, textured works on paper. We met and became friends at Queens College, where she was also getting an MFA in the Art Department. After she received her MFA, she started working as an adjunct professor, and I took her color class. I don't know if I would have taken it if she wasn't teaching it—it wasn't required—but it turned out to be extremely important to me. Color theory is such an important part of my work, so that class is still dear to me. I still have all the books, even. Now, she teaches at the Fashion Institute of Technology.

[35] Louisa Chase (1951–2016) was an American painter and printmaker. After studying art at Syracuse and Yale universities, she moved to New York. Over the course of her career, "the landscape elements and body parts of earlier paintings became enmeshed in thickets of color and skeins of calligraphic lines." See William Grimes, "Louisa Chase, Painter of Geometric Shapes and Body Parts, Dies at 65," *The New York Times*, May 16, 2016, A19.

1/5/80

I finished making three pieces for the Jamaica Arts Center—only more than 36 hours late.

Secondly, I don't like the pieces, but I don't know why.

1) Maybe 26" is too wide. Maybe it should be 20" by some narrower number.
2) The black one with white lines is too high.
3) The blue and yellow one leans too far to the right at top left.

I was depressed last night when I wrote the notes on page 71 (although there were some off placements of the closed fields). I must take pictures this week so I can do some new work. I also have to take some color prints. The opening is Jan. 15 at 5pm (at the Jamaica Arts Center).

I’m getting into drawing again.
I made some small, interesting ones—
Also, I’m excited about using spray paint to make a negative grid. The first came out beautifully, like a photograph.

(I got the spray idea from David Smith.)

I read an excerpt from an interview with Gene Davis.[36] He said something like:

"Just because painting and sculpture have existed so far doesn't mean they will be around forever . . . "

I believe art is certainly earthbound, or bound to some planet, with the exception of literature and definitely music.

I hope that my work is in some sense positive or optimistic. I have no need to speak of the alienation of life, the struggle, the constant horror stories of cruelty and violence done to humans by humans. In fact, these negative realities keep me from making art. If all that lies ahead of humanity is death and destruction which goes on . . . At the same moment, I will not depict the idyllic, because it is also not reality. I believe in the struggle toward emotional and intellectual enlightenment—searching for a change and evolving into, and toward, a more complete person. Maybe when we humans get to that place there will be no need for art as we now know it.

The creativity that occurs in the sciences may replace the physical art object in that the sciences' intellectual rewards may be greater.

[36] Gene Davis (1920–1985) was an American painter and printmaker associated with the Washington Color School of the late 1950s and '60s, as well as a journalist and writer. When asked by Barbara Rose, "What do you think is the difference between, say, stripes in a painting, and stripes in wallpaper design . . . ?" Davis replied: "The only requirement I make of art . . . is that it look good and continue looking good with the passage of time, whether it's a wallpaper or whatever. Maybe wallpaper can be art, too, if it continues to look good. That's quite a demand actually, that something continue to look good forever." See Barbara Rose, "A Conversation with Gene Davis," *Artforum* 9, no. 7 (March 1971): 50.

I did some work—amazing how it makes me feel better.
Did some new sketches for new work.
Remember curvature, I should do something about that.
Must think about the idea but mostly it's an extension of *Seen Twice*.

I am excited by the idea of moving *Seen Twice* to a much larger white field and juxtaposing white on black. Still, only the area within the white can be changed—the black is a natural constant. I am wondering if the figure or the body, as I am calling it, is becoming or has become nonfunctional, its use arbitrary.

I can tell when making a piece that my first concern is the ground. Maybe this has something to do with painting the background.

Maybe I should try using the mesh as the ground.

I also read an article about Joseph Beuys[37] in January's issue of *Artforum*.[38] It was really good, mostly because it has a different (and not entirely positive) point of view.

[37] Joseph Beuys (1921–1986) was a key figure in European avant-garde art during the 1970s and '80s. His avant-garde performances such as How to Explain Pictures to a Dead Hare (1965) contributed to Beuys's "personal mythology." See Ian Chilvers, "Joseph Beuys," in *The Oxford Dictionary of Art and Artists* (Oxford: Oxford University Press, 2009).

[38] Benjamin H. D. Buchloh, "Beuys: The Twilight of the Idol," *Artforum* 18, no. 5 (January 1980): 35–43.

I can definitely say I don't know what I'm doing.

I really hate my new pieces. I think I have fallen off the wagon somewhere. Sometimes I feel more the artist and sometimes I feel very much less the artist. I wish I knew what I am really looking for. I would love to make art,
teach philosophy,
become a lab technologist.

HOWARDENA PINDELL, *Memory: Past*, 1980–81. Acrylic, dye, paper, thread, tempera, photographic transfer, glitter, and powder on canvas, 126 × 84 in (320 × 213.4 cm).

I finally came up with a radically important decision. Since I don't like the work I did two weeks ago, I am going to back up two steps.

Today I am feeling better.
1) I'll finish *Plotted Body*

Must get slides back and send them to Howardena Pindell.[39]

The problem is that if I don't really love what I have done, I don't feel like an artist.
I have realized that my feeling less intellectual and creative has all to do with my level of artistic (intellectual and creative) activity as well as my physical well-being.

[39] Howardena Pindell (1943–) came to visit Just Above Midtown as part of the "Business of Being an Artist" sessions to talk about getting your work exhibited at different venues and what methods one could use, like submitting your work to juried exhibitions and large group exhibitions. I followed her advice and sent out slides. That's when we first met. Many years later, when I was a gallery director at the Bertha V.B. Lederer Gallery in Geneseo, New York, I included a work of hers in a drawing exhibition I was organizing, *Drawn to New York*.
Pindell is known for addressing social inequities from her vantage as a woman artist of color—she "produced several oral and written accounts" on the discriminatory practices of major New York City galleries and museums. In the late 1960s, Pindell's art "focused on the formal properties of light and color, using dots to create illusions of space and to suggest atmosphere." See Joan Marter, "Howardena Pindell," in *The Grove Encyclopedia of American Art* (Oxford: Oxford University Press, 2011).

Last night I didn't do any work. Today's Steven birthday.

Monday is the meeting at my house. Must get film.

Tonight (2/18) the group is coming over to see my work. After complaining I finally did some work.

I'm feeling better about the four newest pieces but still badly about the earlier four from 2/4. They are junk.

I would like the bodies to be more organic with the shapes and grid, but this aluminum mesh is very hard to manipulate by hand. And the fabric mesh doesn't have enough body, and the grid is too tiny. The grass is always greener . . .

Welcome back, Irene!

At the meeting I learned, of course, that I had exaggerated my artistic problems.

I hope I can hold on to this lesson for more than six months.

Jessie was the only one to whom it meant nothing.
The group suggested I go to a large garden supply store for different meshes that may be usable by hand.
The red and yellow is too contained. I will cut it down.

I have mailed the slides to
Artists Space[40];
Bette Stoler[41];
Howardena Pindell;
and the Zabriskie Gallery.[42]

[10] Artists Space was founded in 1972 in downtown Manhattan.
[41] Bette Stoler Gallery was located at 13 White Street in Tribeca.
[42] This gallery, with multiple locations in New York and Paris, was founded by Virginia Zabriskie in 1954.

I got a postcard notice from Artists Space saying they received my slides.
I didn't realize how it worked, but they choose their shows from the slide registry. So now we'll see what happens.

Ellen Sragow[43]
Clinton Hill[44]

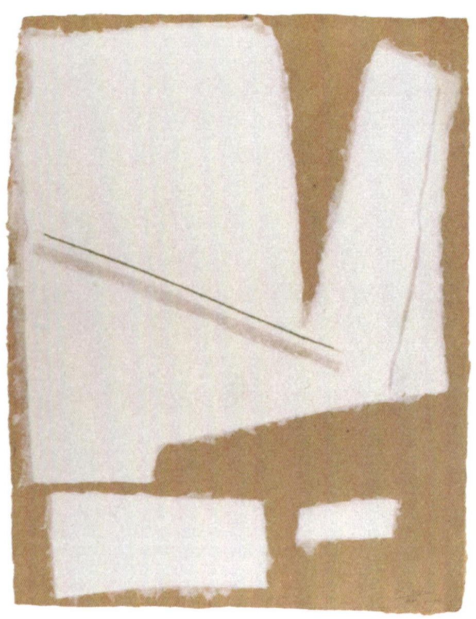

CLINTON HILL, *2*, 1975. Handmade paper, 22½ × 17 in.

[43] Ellen Sragow (1943–2024) was an art dealer who founded her namesake gallery in 1975 in Chelsea, New York.
[44] Clinton Hill (1922–2003) was an artist and my teacher and mentor at Queens College. I remember he gave me some canvas stretchers that had belonged to the abstract expressionist painter, Barnett Newman. I still have them—I can't possibly give them away. In the latter part of his career, Hill "began to incorporate handmade paper and paper pulp into his art practice." His layered artworks "came to resemble relief paintings with strong sculptural qualities that pushed the limits of two-dimensional expressions." See Vanessa Kam, "Announcing the Archive of Visual Artist Clinton Hill," *Stanford Libraries Blog*, August 26, 2019, https://wayback.stanford.edu/was/20201031054642/http://library.stanford.edu/art.

I’m reading about rotating black (Kern) holes and using the diagram of traveling to future universes. I must think it over.

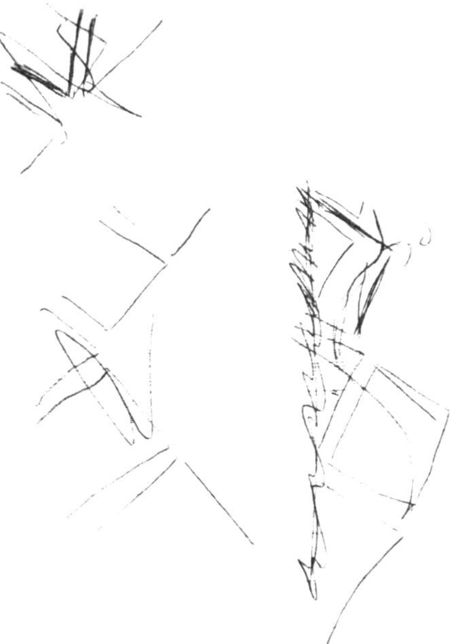

Breaking boundaries—whose boundaries . . .
Nevertheless, I had a vision of a new piece. I am going to break my own boundaries.
In the recent *Seen Twice* pieces, I have been working to the edge of the paper or Masonite, breaking the edge of the white closed field. Now I want to break the outer black edge.

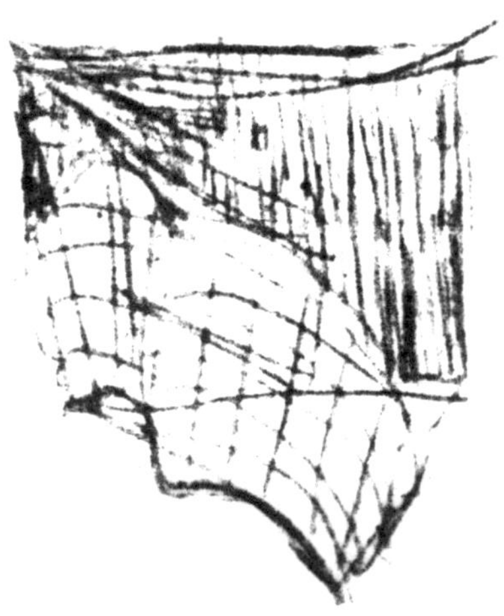

Yesterday (3/18/80) was a good day. I finally completed *Plotted Body*. It's been a year since I first made it in paper.
I started working on the newest pieces—breaking the outer edges, trying to make shapes for the mesh.[45] There is a problem with the mesh. Because the paper shapes are flat, I should exaggerate the curves more. Maybe that would work for the drawings. I should also use the enclosed field with it.

[45] I would cut the mesh using wire-cutters, then shape it using my hands.

It's now April 8th.
The vacation is over. Because of the strike, I haven't been able to go downtown to see anything.

I fell in and out of the writing mood. Writing is difficult, especially if you don't have a deadline for the finished project. Why am I standing here . . .

I started working on *Broken*, or *Breaking Boundaries*. I did one 20” × 26” piece and one 13” × 20” piece.

I need more pliable mesh—that’s for sure—because I want the metal part of the pieces to be more organic. Maybe I can try a non-transparent approach to the grid of *Breaking Boundaries*. I like the smaller one better.
The linear mark studies are somewhat arbitrary.
I think what bothers me most is that they are totally intuitive—is it good or bad to make art in an intuitive way? It is representative of the internalization of what was once basically regimented.

The larger one—I don't know—is either too big or general, or the paper is too big, or the mesh is too big, or the mesh may be too shiny.

The meeting is here tonight.
Do I have much to say?
The only one I really have trouble with is the first big one.
I would like to chop off more paper (put in the little marks).

On Friday, I am going to be interviewed by one Hamilton Brian. This is for a slide show and lecture by the director of the Bronx Museum.

Last Monday I did some new pieces that are much nicer and more like what I had in mind. However, I had a flash during that work period. I saw a piece where the ground part was smaller than the mesh. What this tells me is that the new pieces or the more recent work is becoming more intuitive than it has been for the last two or three years. This is definitely a good sign. I was beginning to feel more restricted in my work, and I am critical of the strict formulaic method used by myself and others that I know. It's really interesting, this creative vacillation.

When your needs as an artist change before you are even conscious of the evolution going on internally . . .

What is my work about?
There is a broad base of concepts, of ideas where neither is more important than the other—for example, to communicate through the visual content of an artwork as well as its intellectual content (that which inspires).

There is a coalescence of the forms of painting and sculpture, bringing the 2nd and 3rd dimensions together. Sculpture can push the dimension of painting further. The newest artwork should be a movement toward some other future form.

Input: information that goes into the artist and becomes art somewhere in the mind.
Acknowledging what goes in and how the input becomes internalized, the artist can leave the formula approach behind. Their intuition can freely use all that input to form the works.

Politics of Art:
How art is political, because it is always an expression of something, a feeling, or an occurrence. Some, and I include myself, feel entrenched in the historicism of formalism. Formalism to my mind is political. Formalism sets up limitations, and most importantly guides how we look at art. I resent art that is obviously formalist. Yet, I wonder if others see my work as pure formalism. Formalism—I am against it, but we are entrenched in it.

The interview took place as scheduled on Friday. Hamilton Brian said it would only take half an hour to forty-five minutes. It lasted two hours. It went well. I was very nervous, but I was also very candid, and I didn't say one thing that I regret. Saturday we (Steven and I) went to SoHo. Liked the Laurie Anderson[46] show at Holly Solomon.[47] Important! Just found Printed Matter[48] and Franklin Furnace.[49] I'll make three books. I want to do one with Steven, one with Judith, and one alone.[50] Manner of approach:

1) Stick to the traditional book form.
2) Book of only images, pictures, and drawings.

[46] Laurie Anderson, *Dark Dogs, American Dreams*, Holly Solomon Gallery, New York, April 12 to May 3, 1980.
People were just beginning to think about sound as an artistic vehicle, and Laurie Anderson's work was challenging and very interesting to me. Much later, I learned about Ben Wigfall (1930–2017), a painter and printmaker who relocated to New York from Virginia. Wigfall had an exhibit at Kenkeleba in the '80s, and showed prints based on audio tapes he recorded about his estranged father's life.

[47] This gallery was founded by Holly Solomon in 1975 and closed in 1999.

[48] Printed Matter is a non-profit bookstore and arts space founded in 1976.

[49] Founded in 1976 by Martha Wilson, the arts organization Franklin Furnace is now part of Pratt Institute, Brooklyn, and The Museum of Modern Art, New York.

[50] Judith Wilson-Pates (1952–) is a historian of African American art. She began her career writing for *Ms. Magazine*, where she wrote a profile of painter Alma Thomas ["Alma Thomas: A One-Woman Art Movement," 1979]. When she turned to painting, she started coming to the Ten Women artists' group meetings. She later earned a PhD in art history from Yale University, where she wrote a dissertation on the artist Bob Thompson. She taught at several universities and retired from the University of California, Irvine, in 2006.

I have written a letter to a Douglas Davis, the author of *Artculture*, which has some exciting essays.[51] I have yet to type it. I want some regular paper.
I would like to get a reply.

[51] Douglas Davis, *Artculture: Essays on the Post-Modern* (New York: Harper & Row, 1977). Douglas Davis (1933–2014) was a new media artist and art critic for Newsweek.

I haven't done any new work since the group was here. But I have written my first essay which I asked Judith to read. I was going to show it to the group, but I have changed my mind. I can't do any work because I haven't taken pictures. That is my fault because I haven't read the camera booklet, which I shall do Sunday night, I hope.

I found out today I have to make two pieces (special).
One is *Primarily Art*, and I must make a second piece for a public art project that Linda is going to set up. Steven gave me a few suggestions. It really is a take on the first idea I had for art in public places: a tall box painted black inside, and people would go through it. But I don't like it because that idea's not safe at night. This is better and safe: a box with circles and squares cut in it, black on the inside with red and yellow stripes. The mesh figures will be over or near the various windows. It will have a disposable fluorescent light or a trap door hatch to let in varying amounts of light. I have to name this piece.

Tonight is June 5, 1980. The gallery Just Above Midtown had a benefit. It was really nice. There were plenty of people, and by the time we left the reception table, we had collected probably a thousand dollars.
The show was fun. My piece was a game, *Primarily Art*. It is spoken of earlier in this journal.

I must say, though, I didn't like the fact that they ran out of beer. They didn't even have hard liquor. But they ran out of beer.

Also, I met Jeff again.[52] I haven't seen him in about seven or eight years. He's a little heavier but he looks the same. He is a wonderful person. We left earlier than we were planning—I don't remember why.

[52] Jeff Segal was my friend at Queens College. He had a longstanding interest in photography.

I have taken the photos of my work. For the first time I took them myself. Steven was a little upset because he feels I was taking away his involvement in my work. But the truth is not that—I want to control the picture process, because too often there are problems like the picture not being centered, which is most of the time.

Today, June 29, 1980, Linda Goode Bryant called to give me the dates of my show.
Solo show, first solo show.
I tried to call members of the group to tell them, but of course no one was home. I'll try again. The dates are January 10–31, 1981.

Today is August 5.
Steven and I went to Montreal, Canada, for ten days. We got back August 1.
I finished the reading I was doing for Simon & Schuster. Now it's time to get to work for my show; I am supposed to call Ms. D'Ste. Armand. Also have to call Linda and Howardena Pindell.

I'm trying a larger piece that will still be minimal in appearance. I personally can't see idea-wise how I, or anyone, can really change or enhance the piece simply by being bigger. Especially if the idea the work is based on is so grand in scale, how can a few feet make the piece more physical? If the idea is to confront the viewer, to challenge the viewer to a duel for space to be in, the actual scale has nothing to do with the scale of the idea.[53]

[53] Now, however, I would say that the physical size of a work does contribute to its impact on the viewer.

I finished the ground of the larger piece. It has lost quite a few inches in the making. I am certainly not interested in making huge pieces because an idea is larger than life.
In addition, why should one write longhand if one can write shorthand? Or take for example a mathematician, or $E = mc^2$. Almost everyone knows what this represents; it does not have to be written to understand what it means.

I have a lot of work to do, but I must find out certain things first:
1) Concerning the space, I have to know how many pieces I'll be able to put in the show.

Oh, this new piece is called *Paths* (named after Robert Frost's poem "The Road Not Taken").[54]

[54] Robert Frost, "The Road Not Taken," in *The Poetry of Robert Frost: The Collected Poems, Complete and Unabridged*, ed. Edward Connery Lathem (New York: Henry Holt, 1979), 105.

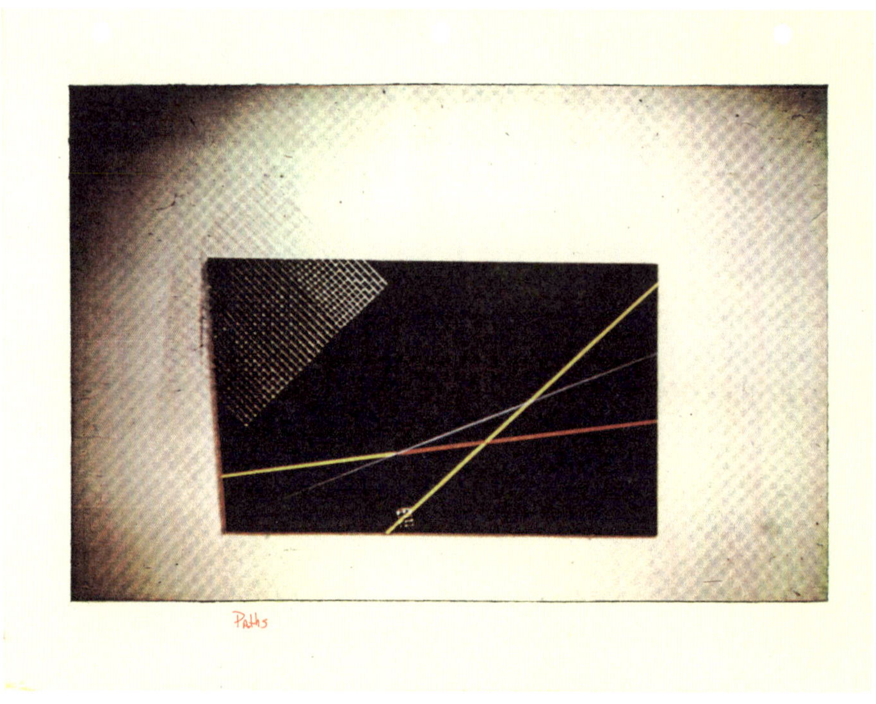

Xerox of a slide of *Paths*, 1980–81. Mixed-media sculpture, 22 × 37½ × 22½ in.

Now it's 8/20 and I've only that half-completed piece *Paths*. I'm having some trouble getting started. This is to be expected after such a long vacation from my work. I want to first find out some things about the paint and how easily it burnishes. I have to buy some supplies.

I also must admit my preoccupation with this freelance reading I've been doing, and my growing concern about my job this fall. I really don't want the job. But it's really whether or not I will be laid off by the Board of Education. I'm impatient, that's the problem. I'm reading *The Confessions of Nat Turner*.[55] I like reading so I'm interested in the possibility of going into the publishing business.

I would like to write one of those silly romance stories for some extra money. But I just don't know if I could keep the story going for a hundred and fifty pages. Maybe later I will give it a try.

[55] William Styron, *The Confessions of Nat Turner* (New York: Random House, 1967).

Today Steven and I had a serious discussion about law school and him in general.

I held back my tears, and he gave into his. This, I think, means something important. I asked him why he can't help himself. He certainly helps everyone else. He asked why he must be the one to do the job. He said that I have the ambition, so why don't I do it?

I finished *Paths*. I didn't and I don't care about it, any of it, right now. Except that when I was sitting here, I got a flash of another possible piece.

It makes me think of a flag.
I want to write, but writing takes such a different kind of concentration.

I'm working on a piece called *Whose Horizon*. I first thought I would complete it at 10.5" by 26". Then I thought maybe I'd make it larger. I like 21" × 52", but I'm trying 10" × 52". The narrowness is very interesting on graph paper, but the divisions may not work out in scale. I will try it first on paper. For this piece I will also use thicker ¼" tape.
I made a paper piece that's 10.5" × 54". It looks alright to me, but it doesn't look like the larger size makes much difference. I'm looking at it right now and it seems to make the horizons, and the title *Whose Horizon* makes more sense.

I wish I knew how many pieces I need for the space because I don't want to go backward—I want to show all new work.

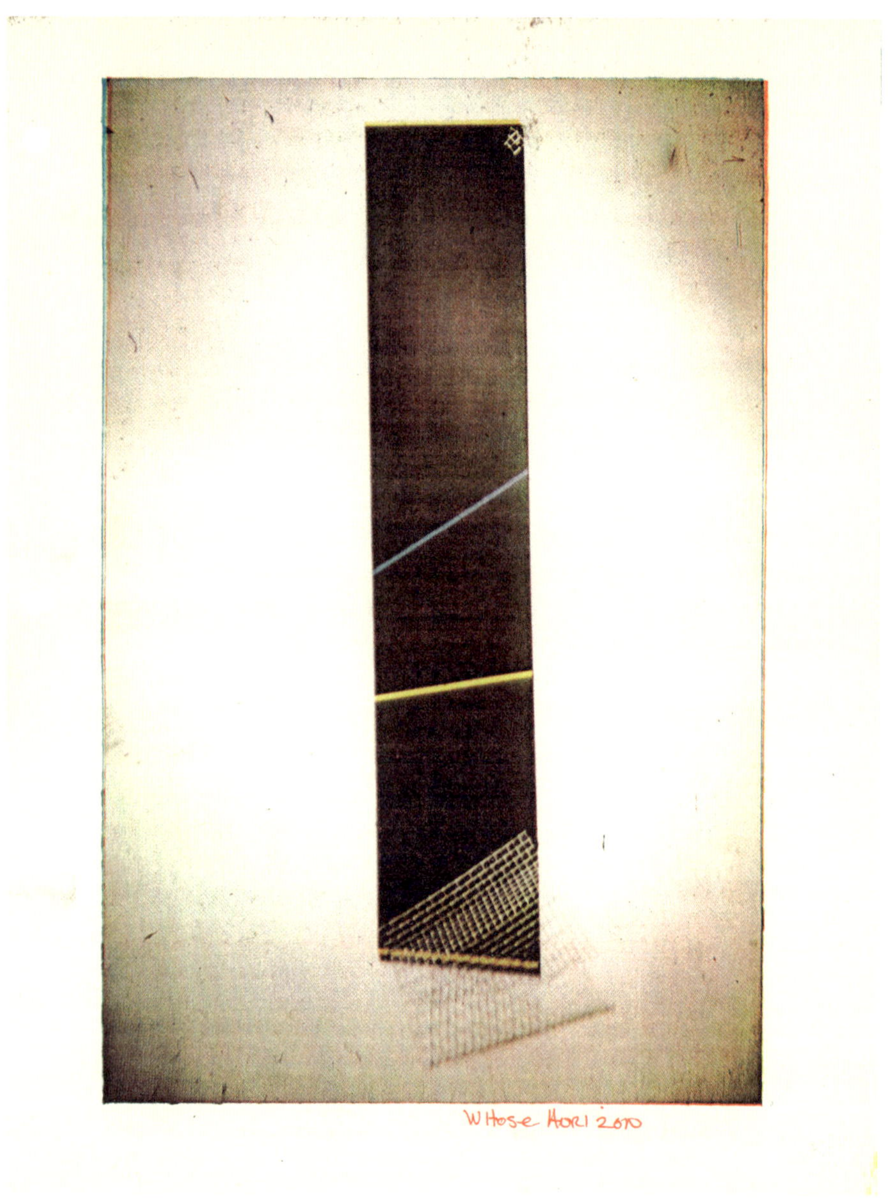

Xerox of a slide of *Whose Horizon*, 1980–81. Mixed-media sculpture, 10½ × 54 × 3 in.

A third new piece is on its way.
My left hand is tired from cutting a long piece of mesh.
This piece has no name, but its idea is to let the viewer feel the rotation of the entire piece, and also to feel bottom heavy (this makes me think of big asses).
Tomorrow I'll pick up some film, then make these three pieces.

I finished *Whirlaround*. I have to look at it for a while.

Questions to ask about my work:

1) Does my work entertain?
2) I no longer feel it is purist.
3) I know my aim is to extend or widen the viewer's horizon.

Looking at the long piece again, I think I'll change the smaller piece at the top.

I am continuing this page because (9/17/80) it's hardly worth it to leave those three piffling lines alone on the page.

I have forgotten again to get film to take pictures. I'm in more than a lazy mood. I'm somewhat overwhelmed by all the anxiety Steven is feeling concerning the applications for law school and studying for the LSAT exam on Oct. 11. I constantly have to reassure him. Somehow my efforts to bolster his confidence seem to backfire sometimes and at the day's end he goes back to his study. It's quite a drain on me. I don't think I can keep doing it.

Everyone else is aware how bright and intelligent he is, except him. He is scared. I would like to know when I am really going to get to work. I have to go to the gallery and see the space. Yesterday we felt a considerable blow. Suffice it to say that I'm going to try to get a two-thousand-dollar loan to make it possible to pay off Steven's student loan so he may be eligible for loans and grants once he gets into law school. Only recently (this evening) has he decided to try again. I hope I can get this money.

While reading "The Size of Non-Size" by Douglas Davis,[56]
I had an idea for a book project called *What Is Art?*
I would send out letters, return envelopes, and a sheet of paper.

The idea is to get a definition of art from an economic and ethnic cross-section, then turn this into a book.

I want to write an essay on scale, on the size of a piece being determined by the scale of the idea.

[56] Davis, "The Size of Non-Size," in *Artculture*, 28–43.

It's September 28th. The meeting was canceled—now it will be Oct. 13th here.

But it's alright because I am feeling better. I will take my slides tonight and send out my first NEA application by Friday.[57]

I fixed two pieces that broke.

The reason for feeling good is because Steven and I had a very good talk about the past three weeks.

9/29
I didn't take the pictures. I am going to paint the walls in here; Steven said the wall looks like a slum.

I got the Masonite and began painting the pieces. This Masonite absorbs the paint more than I remember.
This room looks like a bomb fell. After I do a few pieces, I will clean it up. Almost finished one piece.

[57] The National Endowment for the Arts, a federal agency that offers funding to artists.

I answered Howardena Pindell's letter. She will keep my slides for the registry she is starting.

Next week my application to the NEA will be mailed. I don't know where I am going to keep all these pieces. I will throw away the paper copies of the pieces I finish.

I got a new felt pen. I'm writing with it now. I love pens and sharp pencils.

I got one roll of red tape today. I have to go back Saturday to get some more and some white paint for the two pieces that need white parallelograms.

Tonight I'll complete maybe three pieces. I have to find the hand drill.

I am also timing Steven on his first practice test. I hope he does well!

I will also try to do some drawings for new pieces. If I am lucky, I will take the photos either Saturday or Sunday and get them back Thursday, I hope. Oh yes, I have to get some white paint to do these walls over.

10/2 I am testing Steven, or rather, timing him.

I forgot to call Judy[58] last night but I did call Brenda. As I expected Brenda is taking—as she calls it—a vacation from art. She is leaving the group for a time. How long a time I don't know and neither does she. Suddenly, I feel hesitant about talking about art with her. But her not doing any work doesn't take away or nullify her ability to read work.

Brenda says she gets no pleasure from art—thinking about it, doing it, or even looking at the magazines. I presume that it all frustrates her. I also think her method of transition is that the transition rules her.

[58] Here, Judy refers to Steven Chaiken's sister.

The art rules her. Artmaking is a job, and the job rules her. This job is very difficult because of the really intangible and totally subjective nature of art. Art is an animal that only lives through the human mind and a human sensation that has nothing to do with the body and its sensory experiences.

While I sympathize with her, I can see that her commitment is a weak one. I actually believe that this type of transitional haze can be used as a great time for experimentation. However, I am not the one going through this; all I have said is very easy to say. In addition, I think there are a few other reasons why she is doing this. One, I am sure, is her inability to accept the rejection inherent in taking the work around.

I am afraid too but if I didn’t try to show, I would be very disappointed in myself, in the strength of my work. If I wanted pleasure, I would paint landscapes. For me art has gone far beyond the pleasure I receive from it. Rather, my aims are communicating with others.

A few words about ethnic art:

While waiting for some paint to dry, I fantasized that I would give a lecture at Stony Brook. Why Stony Brook? Because they just opened their new exhibition space, and it is beautiful. In this fantasy someone asks how I feel about what is known as ethnic art, or art by black artists about the black community. I hesitate at this question because what I think about it will not, I assume, go over big with the artists who do this kind of work. My answer: Well, I don't particularly care for folk art. As a matter of fact, it really turns me off. However, there are exceptions, really only one that I can think of, and I don't remember his name. Anyway, I feel that it has a place because some like it.

I feel that for the most part, it is extremely limiting to the artist. I couldn't do it. In some ways it is political and that's good. But for myself it dwells too much in a segmented "here and now."

(I didn't answer the question well at all. In fact, I went completely off the point.)[59]

[59] Like many of my peers at this time, I had the restrictive choice to either identify as a Black artist—and invite a narrow set of assumptions about my work—or insist that I was not a Black artist, but simply an artist.

I didn't look back to see if I mentioned I was having trouble with one piece, *Seen Twice #7*. The white paint kept cracking—hairline cracks—and no matter how many times I paint it, the cracks still show up. Now I just finished scraping and sanding it. I'm painting it again. I'll see now if the cracks reappear.

Last night I spoke to Judy Wilson.
She spoke to Adrian Piper[60]—a telephone interview for an article she is writing for *Essence*.
I am going to write her a letter.
I just wrote the letter, it is short.
I'm waiting for the surface to dry. May it work this time!

Between Steven's studying for the LSAT and this one piece with the white, I feel like I am being tortured.
I want to take a nap.

[60] Adrian Piper (1948–) is an American mixed-media artist, writer, and philosopher. I first came across her work at Printed Matter. I used to go periodically, and there I found a little book of writings about various public performances she had done.

I finally cut the two straight cuts. Each took about twenty minutes with an X-Acto blade. There was nothing.

10/8
I still haven't taken pictures yet. Painting the Masonite has become an ordeal. I haven't finished any of the new pieces. The meeting is here Monday. This room is too small. But there is nothing I can do about it. I feel really slow-moving; I need to do some stuff in the living room. I decided after the show I'm going to do some writing and work on my new project. I can't work this way. I finished these two, but the rest I'm going to do the old way. This way is getting me down.

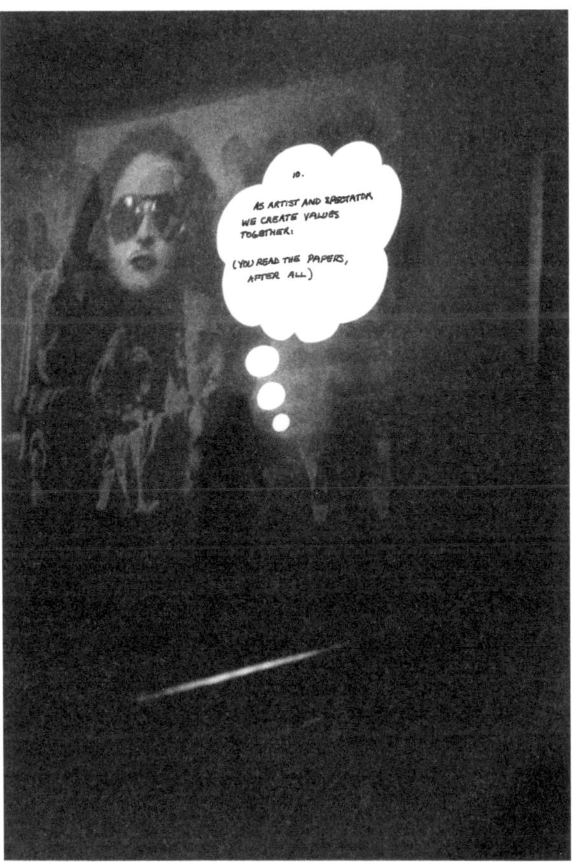

ADRIAN PIPER, *It's Just Art*, 1980. Performance documentation: B&W offset poster, 10 13⁄16 × 14 1⁄8 in (27.5 × 35.9 cm); performance diagram, 8 × 11 in (20.9 × 27.9 cm); 15 silver gelatin photographs on baryte paper with handwritten texts, 11 13⁄16 × 8 ¼ in (30 × 21 cm); 3 collages with handwritten texts, 10 × 8 in (25.4 × 20.3 cm); video reconstruction of performance elements, 00:24:44. Detail: Photo #10 of 15. #80002.1–20.

10/10

The flat enamel worked out wonderfully. It gives me a sense of velvet.

The newer paintings are drying now with brackets in place. I am definitely relieved. I must admit Steven helped me out of my anxiety.

Tomorrow I will drill the holes and find some fishing line, which Fred told me about.[61]

I'll take pictures tomorrow or Sunday. I think the meeting will be in the living room. On Tuesday I'll start working on new pieces.

[61] Fred Wilson worked at Just Above Midtown, the gallery where I exhibited my work in 1980 and 1981, and later as the director at the Longwood Arts Project in the Bronx starting in 1985. I remember an early work he made, a lateral relief sculpture, which had to do with Muhammad Ali—it was shown at Artists Space, in an exhibition I was also included in [*Ali on the Beach*, 1985, painted wood, 6 × 12 × 24 ft, included in the exhibition *Selections from the Artists File*, curated by Kellie Jones, October 1–31, 1987].

I just noticed that Douglas Davis has a show up at P.S. 1.[62] I must get there to see it. I would also like to see the Met's Nigerian show.[63]

I have to get some art magazines to entertain myself.

The glue is not drying. It must be the humidity.

10/12

I am now behind schedule once again. I forgot that I had to mix the epoxy, so I had to do it over. So I will take pictures tomorrow or maybe tonight.

I also have two new pieces planned. I keep forgetting that the group is coming here Monday. And I have to call Irene and remind her to bring the tape recorder.

[62] *Special Projects* (group exhibition), P.S. 1 Contemporary Art Center, Long Island City, Queens, New York, September 28 to November 9, 1980.
[63] *Treasures of Ancient Nigeria: Legacy of 2,000 Years*, Metropolitan Museum of Art, New York, August 14 to October 26, 1980.

Now I'm thinking about what I will say to the group about my work. As of this moment, I have no problems, just the procedure, which I have resolved. I can show them the newest drawings.

Well, the meeting was nice. Vivian told me to spray with a matte varnish or spray.[64]
On *Paths* they thought the larger mesh might be too big.

They said the new drawings seem to be very big—all of them, but especially the first one.

They also said I should find out exactly what space is available to me. I'll do that tomorrow. I will call Linda first chance, after ten o'clock.

The group is definitely valuable. But I don't know how long it is going to last.
Maybe it should be fought for.

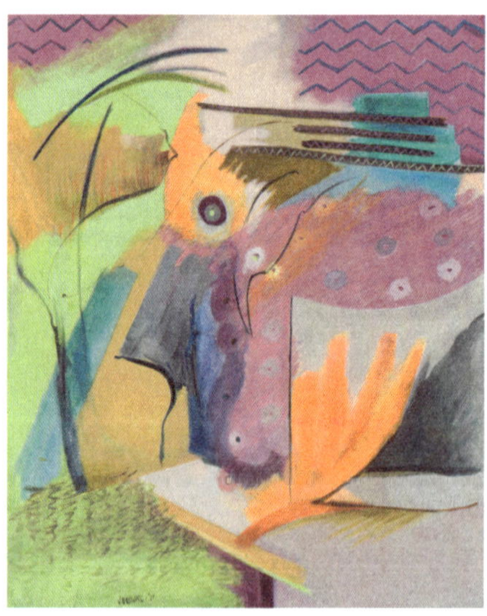

VIVIAN BROWNE, *Umbrella Plant*, 1971.
Oil on canvas, 48 ¾ × 40 ¾ in.

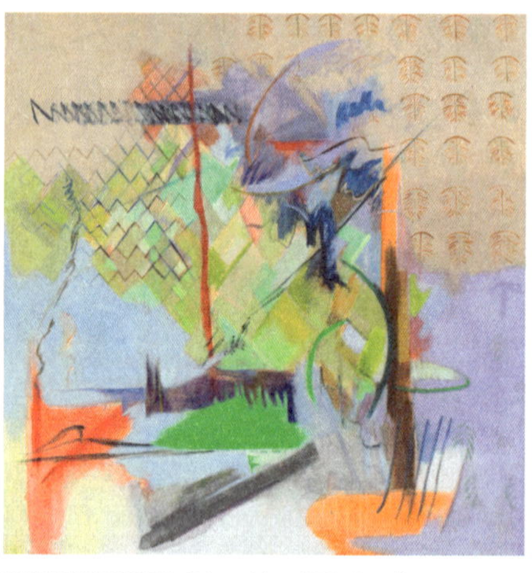

VIVIAN BROWNE, *Diversities*, 1973. Acrylic on canvas, 54 ¾ × 54 ¾ in.

[64] Vivian Browne (1929–1993) was an American painter and a friend. In my mind, she was an abstract painter, though most of her work is figurative. Raised in New York, she studied at Hunter College and later at the University of Ibadan in Nigeria before teaching fine arts at Rutgers University. She was a member of the feminist collective Heresies as well as the Feminist Institute, the first women's art school in New York. I especially liked her *Africa Series* (1971–74), which she made after her trip to Africa.

10/14

Spoke to Janet today.[65] I found out that I have to get black-and-white photos for the invitations.

I got Sandra's number to talk about space.[66]

The application will have one year's worth of slides and my new resume.[67]

Must get photos as soon as possible.
I wondered if the photo should be matte or glossy. It should be glossy.

10/15

I mailed the application last night.

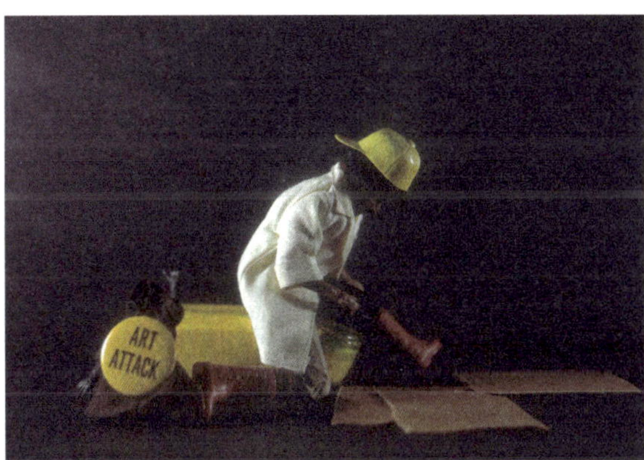

JANET OLIVIA HENRY, *Ritual: Art Attack*, 1982–83. Diorama, mixed-media installation with toys and dolls (Mego Lieutenant Uhura from Star Trek action figure with make-up removed wearing a yellow Mego baseball cap, ¾-length ecru shirt, yellow sleeveless blouse, beige knee-high overalls, dark brown nylon socks, brown ochre plastic cowboy boots; and black screaming rubber chimpanzee wearing Star Wars Jawas monk's habit and Art Attack buttons); Japanese handmade brown rice paper; and Pelikan fountain pen glass inkwell. Dimensions variable.

[65] Janet Olivia Henry (1947–) is a Queens-based mixed-media artist. Henry studied art at the School of Visual Arts and the Fashion Institute of Technology. With Linda Goode Bryant, Henry produced *Black Currant*, a magazine highlighting the experimental work of artists who were showcased by Just Above Midtown Gallery (JAM). I enjoyed interacting with Janet and loved her sense of humor and her work, including her work on *Black Currant*, which I found impressive. Years later, in March 2003, I exhibited her work at Tompkins College Center Gallery at Cedar Crest College in Allentown, Pennsylvania.
[66] Sandra Payne (1951–2021) was an American artist working primarily in collage. We had concurrent solo shows at Just Above Midtown in 1981. Our work went well together in that show; I liked her hand signs and signals, which were textural in a way that addressed sign language and had a graphical interface. She was a librarian at the New York Public Library.
[67] My application for the NEA.

10/18/81

I had planned to go to the gallery this morning before Sue and Charles came over, but needless to say, I couldn't get out of bed.

So here I am planning the trip for next weekend.

10/19

I forgot to mention that my name appeared in *Art in America*. Judy Wilson was very clever in the way she got my name in. However, it was very exciting. I showed the paragraph to everyone. I would like to send the letter to Adrian Piper. I want to establish a rapport with her. Why? I guess because her work is so radically different from mine, from anyone I know about.

I spoke to Cynthia G. It wasn't a very interesting conversation. I expect to find her more up. Maybe it was me, I don't know. Jessica is back—she's doing textile design for Halston.
This also sounds very exciting. However, she isn't doing any work. Artwork that is. That leaves me and Angela.[68] Vivian is not staying in the group because of the time involved. So, after talking to Jessie, I agree that we should hold off on new people until the holidays have passed. She is going to call Irene and tell her herself.

[68] Angela may refer to one of my peers at Queens College, or to an older artist who joined our group for around six months.

I have made three more drawings. I like them.

With the first one, I think I am going to spray paint a white grid on the area designated A.

These three are smaller: the largest side is $4\ {}^{4}/_{8}$”.

I’ll say this: Steven’s application process gives me more time to work. I mean I wouldn’t normally work so late under ordinary circumstances. So now I have eighteen pieces. I may have to replace some of the *Seen Twice* pieces with these new pieces because I don’t have enough space. I wouldn’t mind it at all.

10/21/80

Last night I spoke to Margaret Thatcher.[69] She told me last Friday that she, Richard, and Alistair[70] and his girlfriend went to JAM to see a performance that they were, or rather *are*, having on Friday evenings as part of the dialogue show.[71] They will be going on until November. Margaret told me she didn't like what she saw. She said the two that were very dancelike were particularly bad—mind you, not the worst she has ever seen, but nonetheless bad. Margaret went on to say that she thought JAM has a good chance of getting a large audience for performance work, but that JAM has to be more selective with its choices.

[69] Margaret Thatcher worked at the Dia Art Foundation and became Vice President. We were good friends, actually. After Heiner Friedrich was no longer involved, Thatcher founded her gallery in Chelsea, New York, in 1997. Her husband, Richard, is a conceptual artist.

[70] Alistair was a friend of Margaret and Richard Thatcher's and a successful sculptor. He taught in the art department at Lafayette College in Eaton, Pennsylvania.

[71] *Dialogues* (group exhibition), Just Above Midtown Gallery, New York, October 4 to November 1, 1980.

Well, in answer, I called Linda today and she told me that these performance choices were not made by her; they were chosen by various galleries (fifteen, I think she said) that were involved in the show.
But Linda said she wants to keep the performance as an ongoing part of the gallery. She told me that tomorrow she would be meeting her board of directors to see about getting the second floor. Linda also said that there would be a committee to pick the performance pieces to be shown. All in all, Linda was very happy to hear the feedback and said she would like to talk to Margaret about it.
When I told Margaret this, that Linda wanted to talk about it, she was very excited.

I should also mention that I took the black-and-white pictures myself. It took a long time and I only had twenty exposures. I took pictures of only two pieces, *Paths* and *Untitled: Swing-Time*, as the photo for my invitation.

I also typed my resume. It looks nice and clean. Somehow I thought it would be two pages, but no such luck, only one page. I hope the photos will be ready for Friday, but I doubt it.

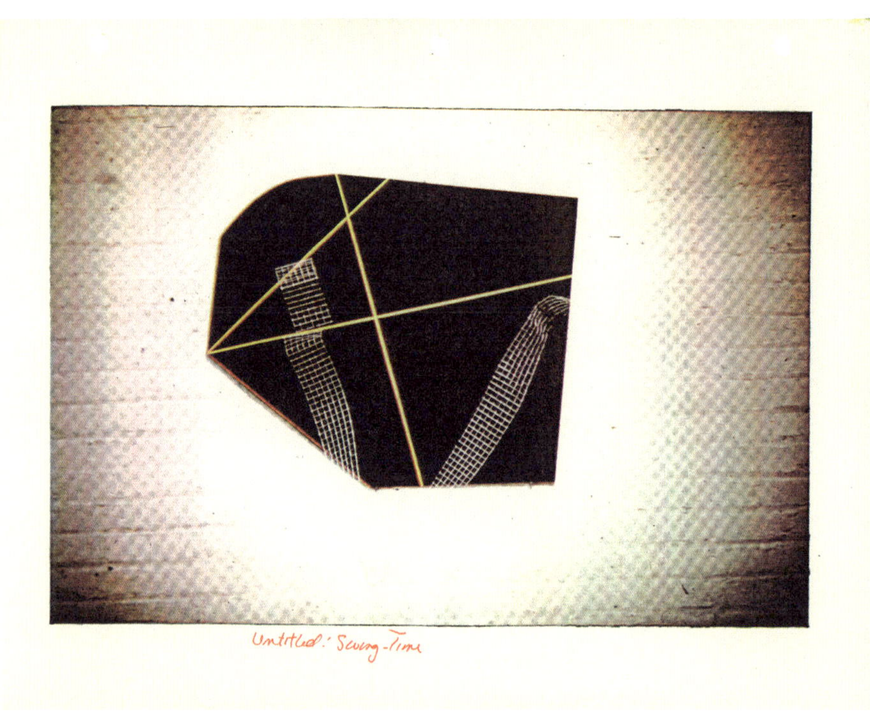

Xerox of a slide of *Untitled: Swing-Time*, 1980–81. Mixed-media sculpture, dimensions unknown.

I am taking the day off. Tomorrow the proof photos come back. If they are any good, then I can relax about it. I have decided to mail the photos because they will get there before next Saturday. I think I'll only get twenty-five copies on really nice paper. I am actually taking Friday and Saturday off as well—I need a break.

Must get some monofilament.

10/24/80

I am intensely proud of myself. The black-and-white came out beautifully.

Today I found out that Audrey Hirsch is dead.[72] She died a month ago. I have to say, I was very shocked. I feel so badly. We were good friends for a long time before the break. It was a nasty occurrence, and it didn't have to happen. Everybody in the group knows. Everyone is hurt by it and feels bad, really bad. Irene tried to call Vic (Audrey's husband), but he wasn't home. There was an obituary notice in *Art Speak* dated Sept 25, 1980. This is horrible.

I was thinking the other day how now I am (we are) old enough to experience people, friends dying. This is hard. It's strange when all of a sudden you know people who are also old enough to die.

[72] Audrey Hirsch (—1980) was a ceramic sculptor and my peer at Queens College. She was part of the Ten Women artists' group until she decided to break away on her own. She had a studio in SoHo. Audrey was very talented, but only had the chance to exhibit in a few group shows. She lived in Queens.

I wish that Audrey hadn't been so crazy. We would all have been friends.

But Irene said that maybe the chemical changes that were happening made her say very weird things on the night that she made me hate her. It's too bad she had to hurt us in order to quit the group. Now she is gone. Goodbye, Audrey. I did love you dearly.

10/29/80

I have made eight drawings plus the four 8 × 10" photos for the invitation. After all this I think I am going to use a close-up photo.
I don't know when I am going to get the Masonite. I should just make the plans myself.
I am also going to need more mesh.

10/30/80

The Masonite was ordered today, so I will pick it up Friday. I also have to get the photos and Steven's jacket; there'll be no time for shopping tomorrow. Saturday I will go to the gallery. Then I will be ready to get everything on the road—

10/31

The Masonite wasn't ready, so I have to get it tomorrow afternoon. The 8 × 10s don't look so great to me. The one close-up is still a contender along with the drawings, which are going downtown tomorrow.

I finally picked up the Masonite.
I also received the floor plan for the gallery.
I find that I can only use the newest pieces plus *Plotted Body*, which amounts to about twelve pieces. And maybe two very small pieces.
I have to speak to Sandra Payne about the space. I want to know what she needs.

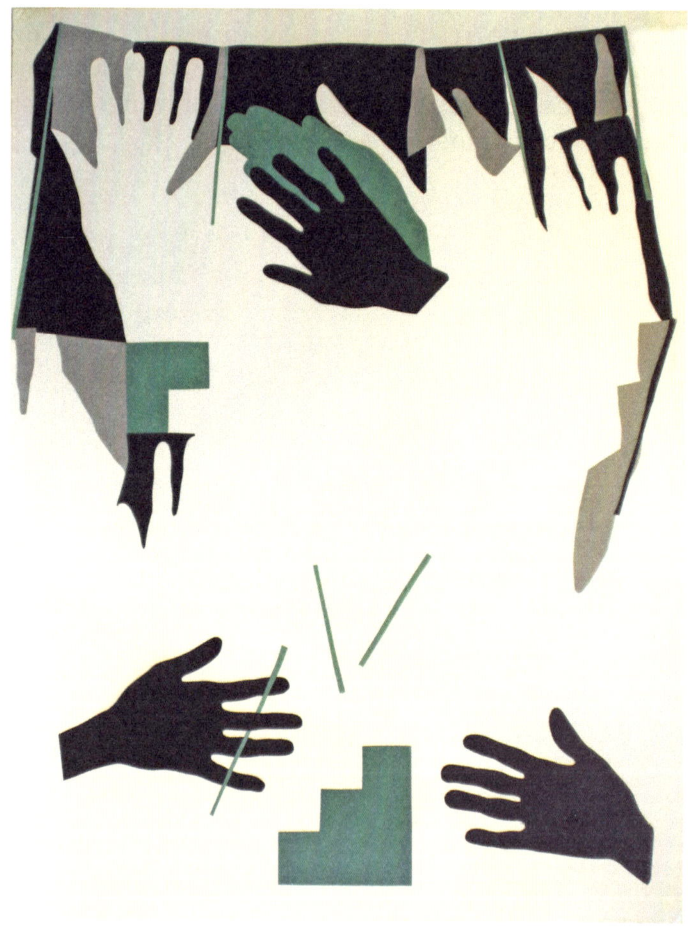

SANDRA PAYNE, *Continental Divide*, 1970. Collage on Rives BFK paper, 30 × 23 in.

I called Sandra Payne and told her about the space. She was very amenable about the space I had chosen. I wonder if I short-changed myself. I don't think so—I want my work all together in that area.

I think I could have filled the space myself. Next time I will.

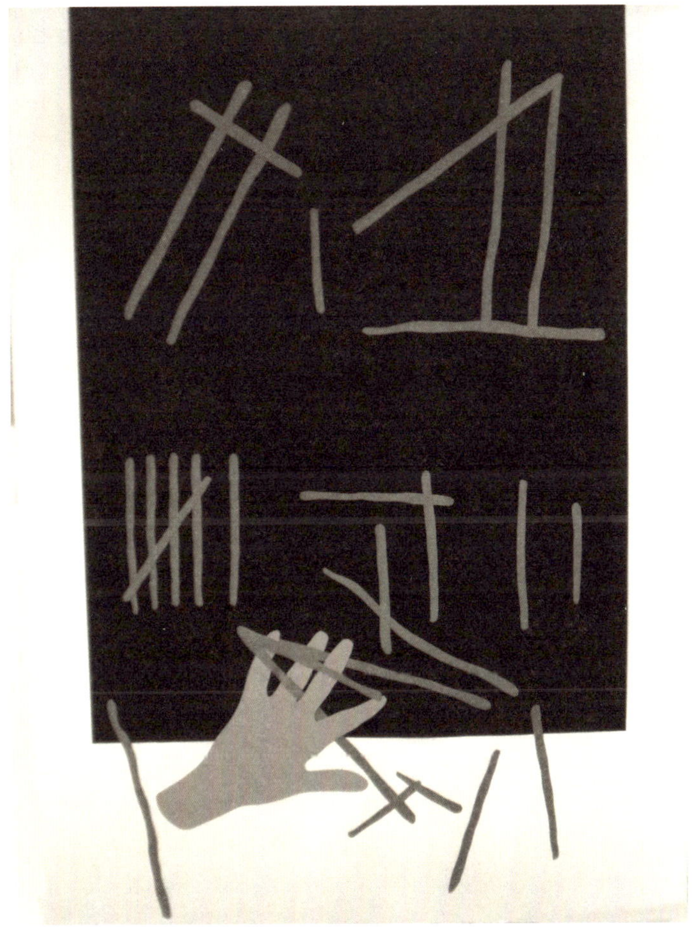

SANDRA PAYNE, *Formula for Madame C.J. Walker's Satin Press Creme Press*, 1980. Collage on Rives BFK paper, 30 × 23 in.

I went to see Jim Turrell's show at the Whitney Museum.[73] There were three pieces that were interesting, one of which really did remind me of Richard Thatcher's *Censored Information*, work that sometimes blocks out the screen.

However, I did like the show, and I will see it again.

The Edward Hopper show was very nice.[74] It's true that Hopper understands morning and evening light like no one else. But you must keep in mind that the painting is done from black-and-white drawings, thereby allowing him to exaggerate the intensity of the light. This also makes his color choices arbitrary, synthetic, and intellectual. This not a judgment, but a fact.

[73] *James Turrell: Light and Space*, Whitney Museum of American Art, New York, October 22, 1980 to January 1, 1981.
James Turrell (1943–) is an American Light and Space artist. I remember that at his first major exhibition in New York at the Whitney, people actually fell through his works, in which the light and color created the illusion of a wall or solid where there was none.
[74] *Edward Hopper: The Art and the Artist*, Whitney Museum of American Art, New York, September 23, 1980 to January 18, 1981.
Edward Hopper (1882–1967) was an American realist painter who worked as a commercial illustrator in New York before fully devoting himself to painting scenes of urban life and domestic interiors where the everyday becomes introspective, mysterious, and estranged.

Back to Turrell: two of the pieces I thought were quite flat, the corner pieces, and this leaning tower of light also seems quite false to me. But all in all, the three larger pieces were, I felt, the most successful.

Reagan is going to be President.

I raised some of the pieces and I painted three small pieces.[75]

11/5/80

This is going to be slow going because I don't have room to paint more than one large piece at a time, and there are six large pieces. I would like to finish the three small pieces tonight, but I have to wait and see how they dry.

[75] I may have raised some pieces off my apartment floor because I was running out of workspace.

Tomorrow at work I will try some shipping companies to ask about a price for a hundred feet or fifty feet.[76]

I am waiting for the stuff to dry up here in the loft and listening to the radio. Oh, I called Janet Henry. She and the layout designer decided on the sprayed black grid with white markings, which was the nicest. I am happy about it—"excited" would be more like it.
Janet also said that we have to be on the offensive with Reagan. He's the oldest president we have ever had.
A man on the news said, "he will probably be taking a lot of naps."

[76] I needed to transport my artwork for the show at Just Above Midtown.

11/6

I called; Janet answered. Reine was not there, but she said that Iris should call and make an appointment to see Reine.[77] Janet is going away after Saturday.

I finished *Little Triangle* and wrapped it up. I also had to repaint the other two triangles.
I might have just enough time to finish these seven new pieces. This is going slowly, especially the painting, because there has been too much turpentine in the brush, and it leaves shiny marks after it dries. Since I am going to be painting every night for a while, I'm not going to clean brushes every night. But I will wrap it in foil to keep the air from it.

[77] Reine Hauser is a writer who worked at Just Above Midtown.

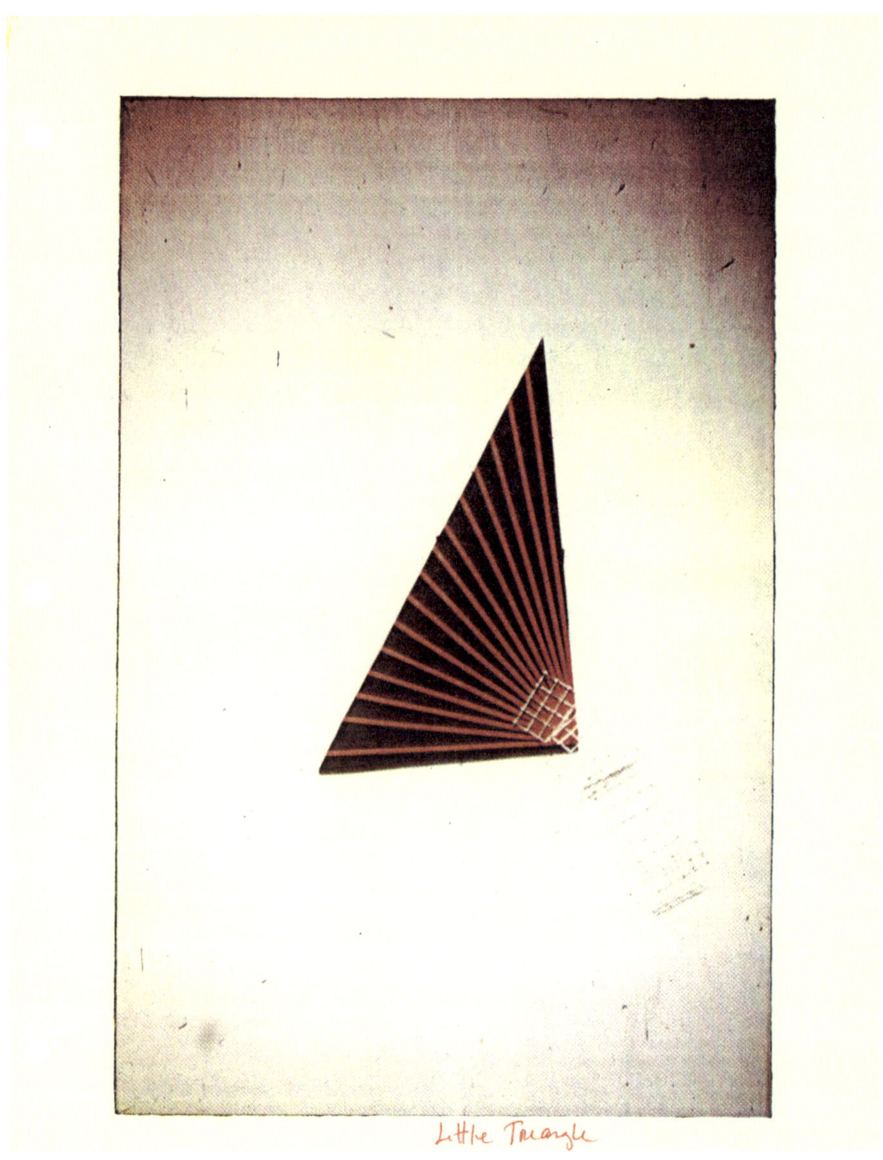

Xerox of a slide of *Little Triangle*, 1980–81. Mixed-media sculpture, dimensions unknown.

I feel badly because if I painted it the right way, I would have two pieces finished tonight.

11/7
I neglected to mention that I am spraying two new pieces with matte finish, which Vivian Browne suggested I do to cure the burnishing problem I had. It leaves a nice finish, a very nice finish.

Yesterday (11/15) I finally got the colored paint, gloves, and the rest. I decided to work only during the week. What I forgot was a new drill bit at 1/32". I am going to call Janet tomorrow to find out about the invitation.

11/20
For one thing, this pen needs to be cleaned.
The work is going slowly and most of it is my fault. But some of the blame lies in the fact that Judy has been here a lot typing. I can't work through a lot of noise and interruptions and Steven's nervousness. I was going to paint tonight but I can't subject Judy to the fumes of the paint.

11/24

Here I have to admit my easy avoidance of work. So I've had one or two problems, but I am letting them get me down. Why, I am being very lazy. Every time I say tomorrow, it ends up being a week before I get started again. Now that Steven's work is completed you would think I could easily get down to work, but there . . .

After some goading, I painted two larger pieces black—*Is this the way to the North Star* and *Universe - Y*.

I have got to call Angela to find out about Monday night. I forgot to ask Irene if she knows where to get flexible cardboard.

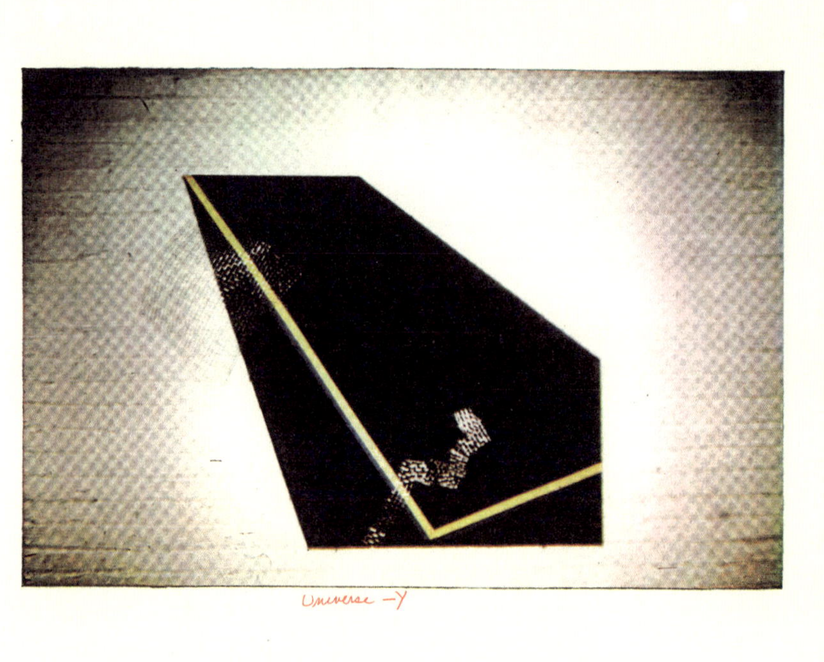

Xerox of a slide of *Universe - Y*, 1980–81. Mixed-media sculpture, dimensions unknown.

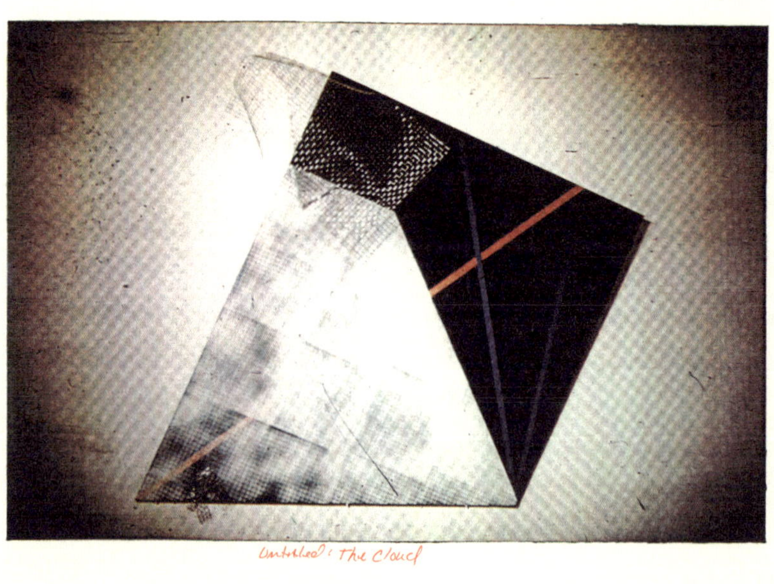

Xerox of a slide of *Untitled: The Cloud*, 1980–81. Mixed-media sculpture, dimensions unknown.

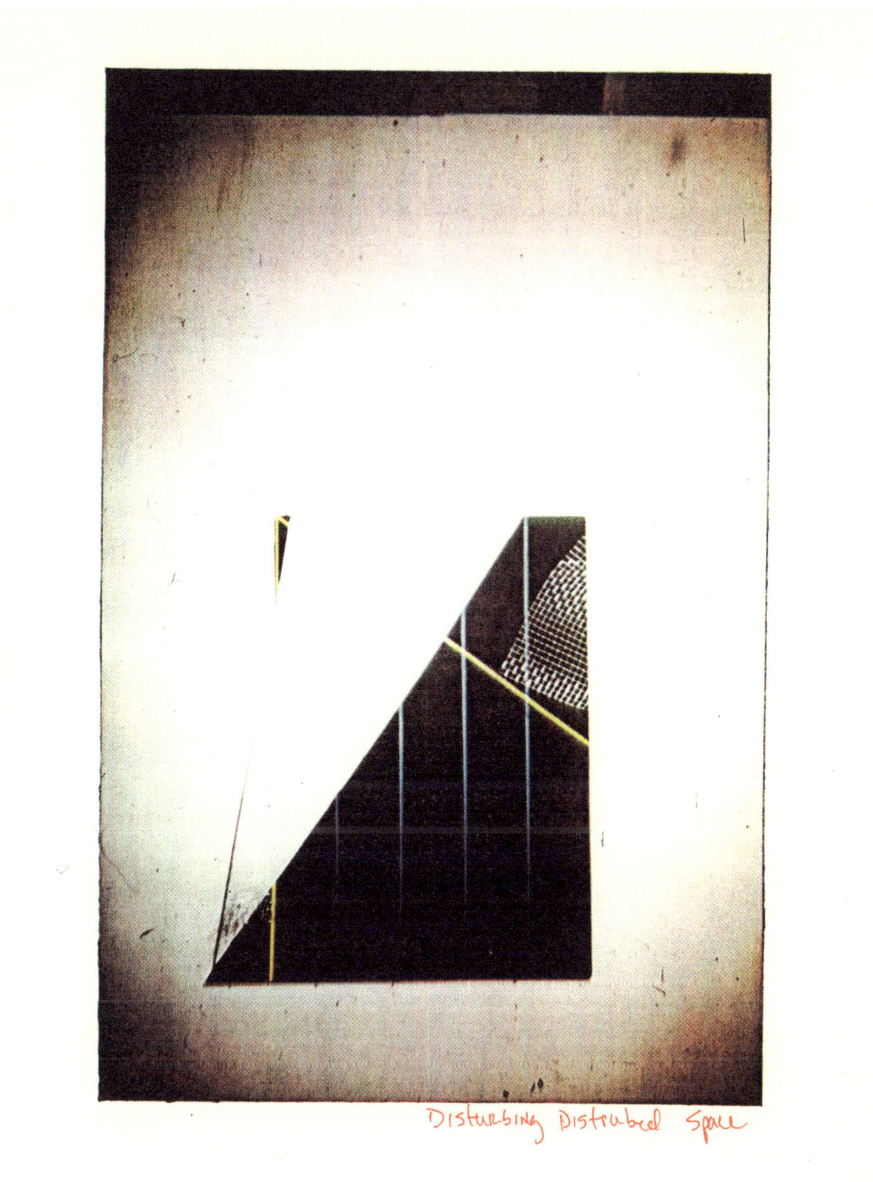

Xerox of a slide of *Disturbing Disturbed Space*, 1980–81. Mixed-media sculpture, dimensions unknown.

11/25

I found out I can use latex on top of flat enamel. So that's what I bought.

I received the acknowledgement from NEA.

I also got a notice from Artists Space to update my file there by December 1st or as soon as possible because they have a new director, Linda Shearer.[78]
I have a new book, a blue one to continue notes.

[78] Linda Shearer (1946–) was the Executive Director of Artists Space from 1980 to 1985.

1981

January 10-31, 1981
Solo exhibition at Just Above Midtown

Facing:
Exhibition postcard for *Cynthia Hawkins / Sandra Payne*, Just Above Midtown, New York, January 10–31, 1981.

pp. 158–159
Cynthia Hawkins (left) and Sandra Payne (right) at the opening of *Cynthia Hawkins / Sandra Payne*, Just Above Midtown, New York, January 10–31, 1981.
Works pictured, from left to right: *Paths*; *Vue Deux Fois #7*; (above) *Little Triangle*, (below) *Vue Deux Fois #6*; *Whose Horizon*.

pp. 160–161
Vivian Brown (left) and Cynthia Hawkins (right) in conversation among the crowd at the opening of *Cynthia Hawkins / Sandra Payne*, Just Above Midtown, New York, January 10–31, 1981.

pp. 162–163
Installation view, *Cynthia Hawkins / Sandra Payne*, Just Above Midtown, New York, January 10–31, 1981.
Works pictured, from left to right: *Vue Deux Fois #2*; *Vue Deux Fois #3*; *Vue Deux Fois #4*; *Vue Deux Fois #5*; (facing wall) *Untitled: The Cloud*.

CYNTHIA HAWKINS

SANDRA PAYNE

solo exhibition
january 10, 1981 / january 31, 1981

opening reception
saturday, january 10, 1981
3-5 pm

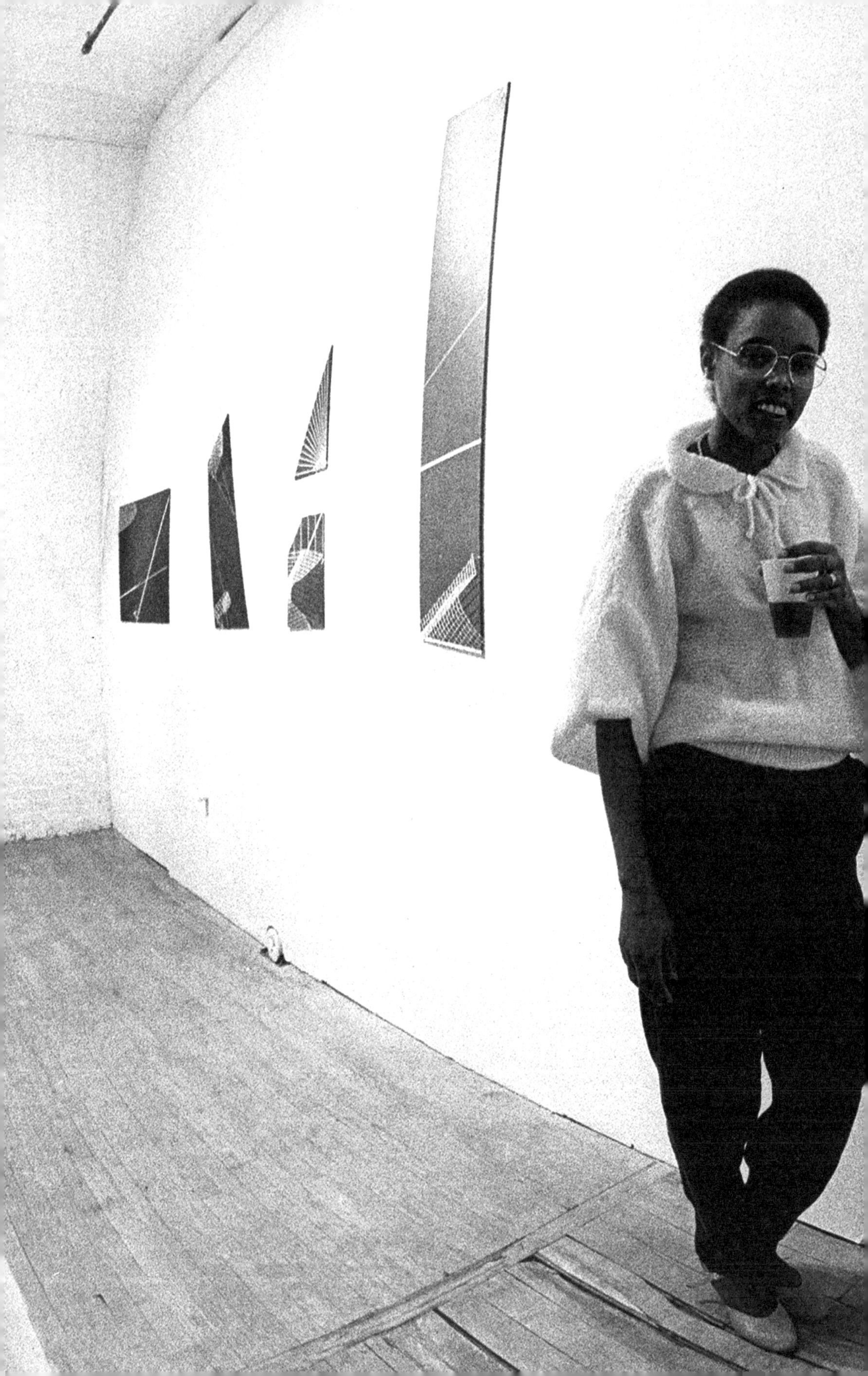

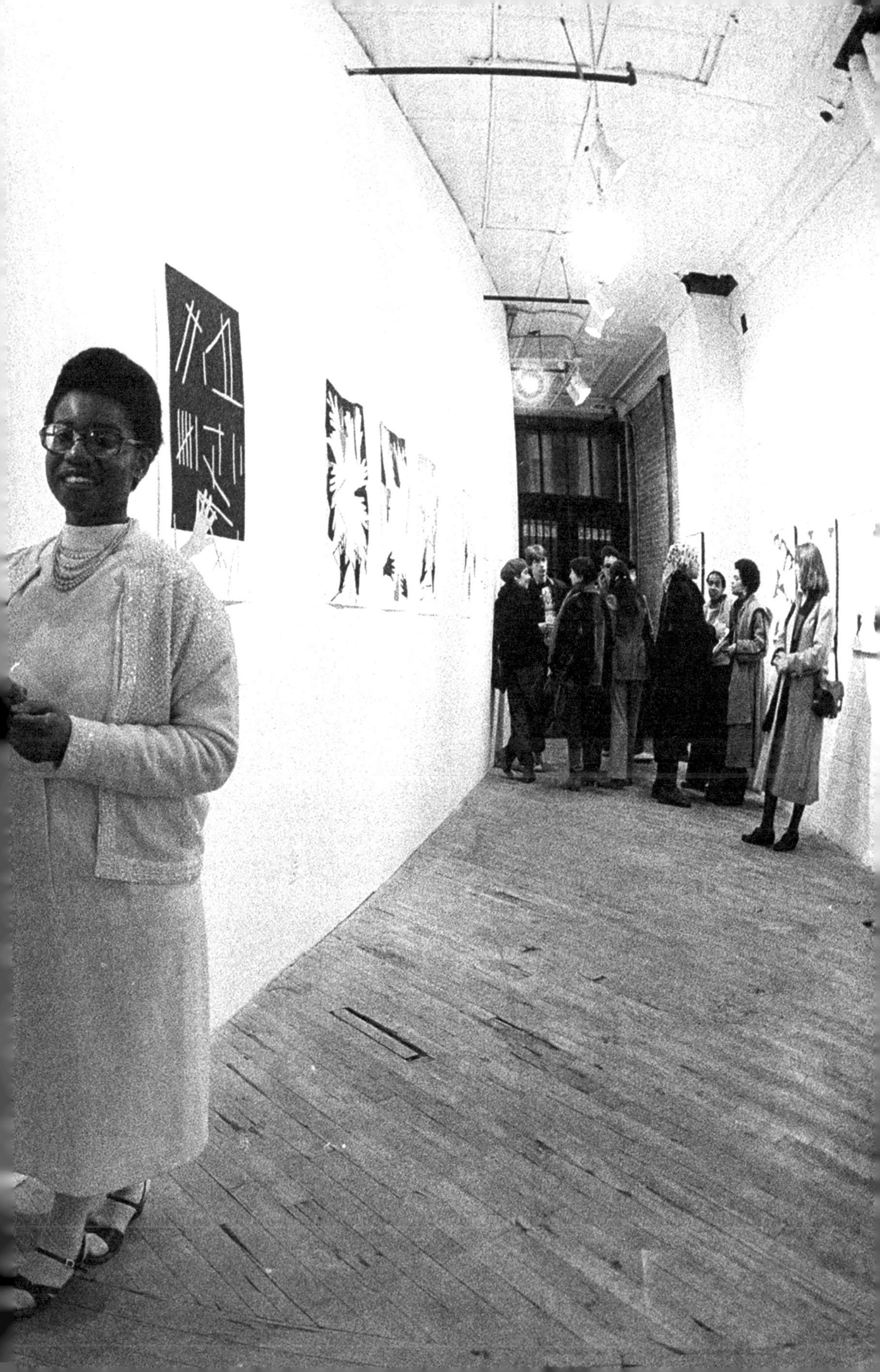

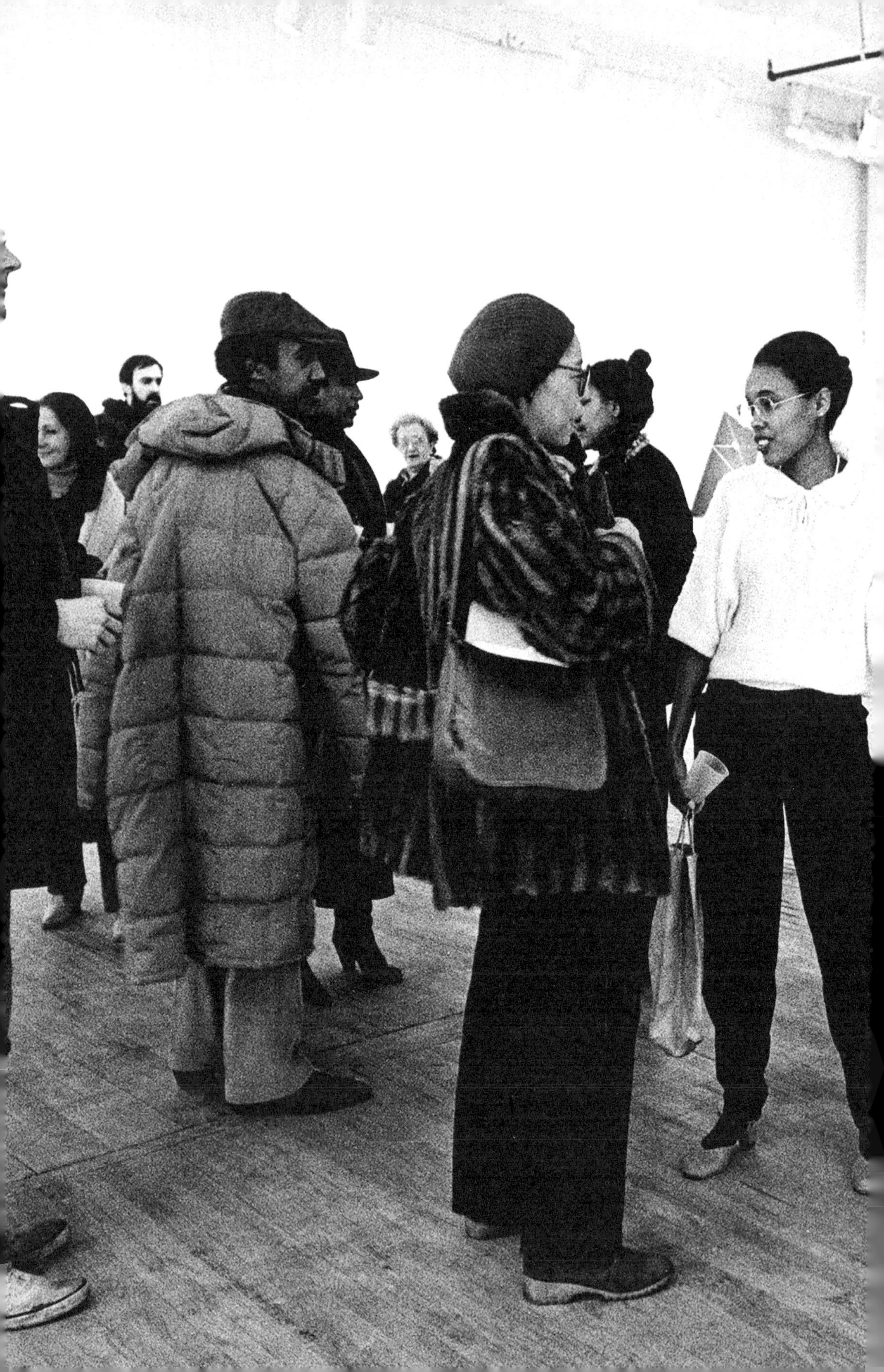

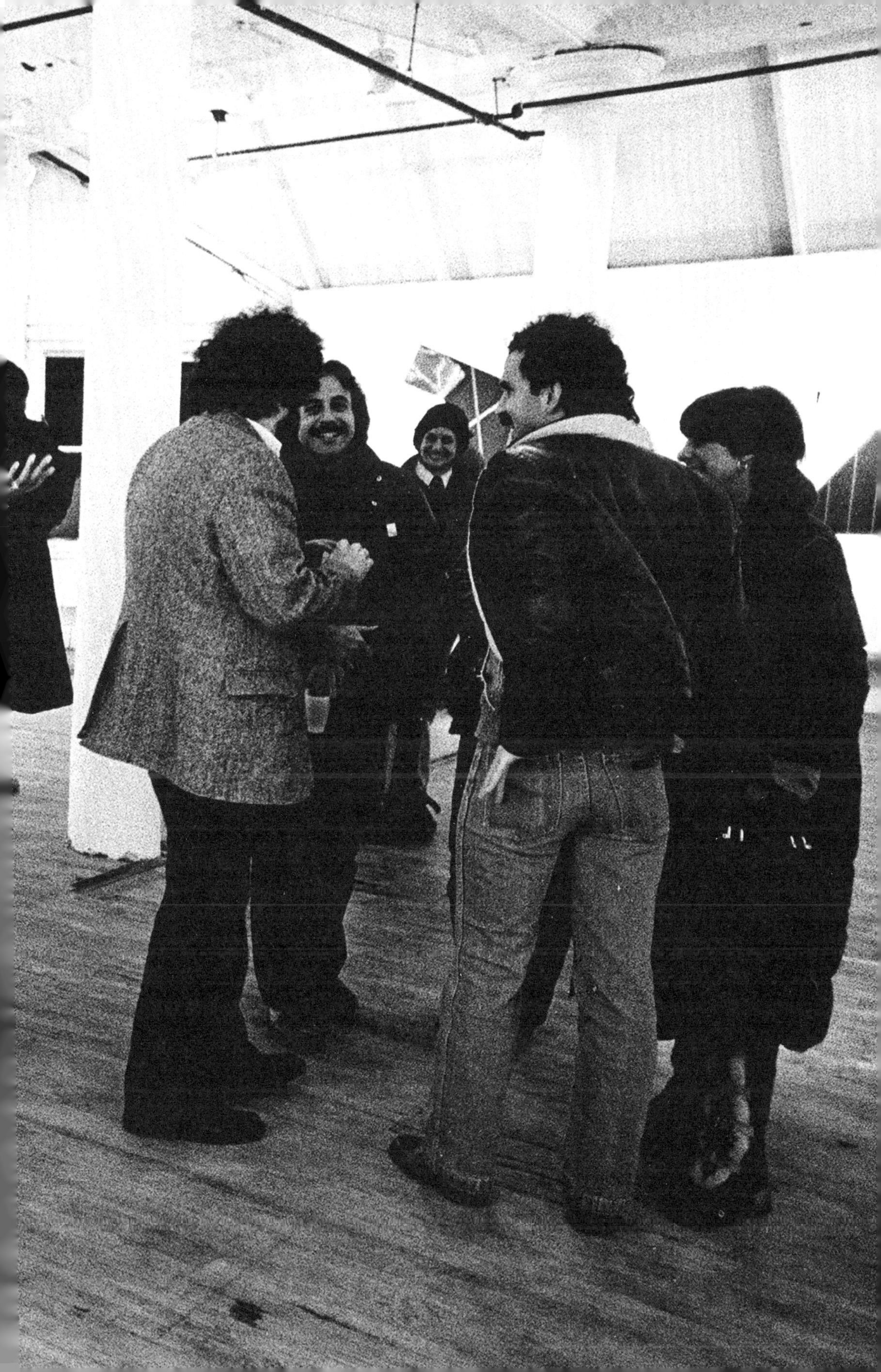

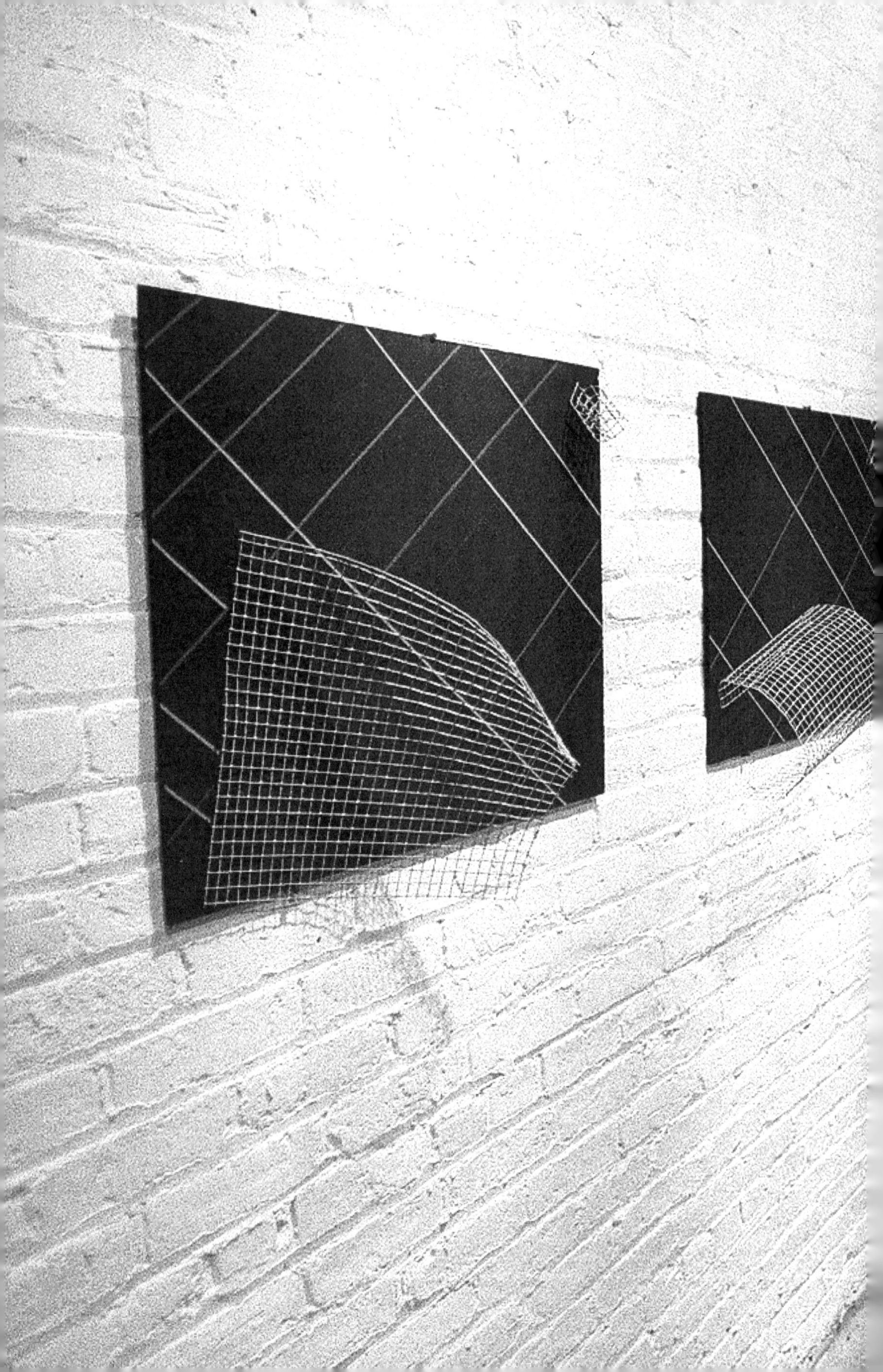

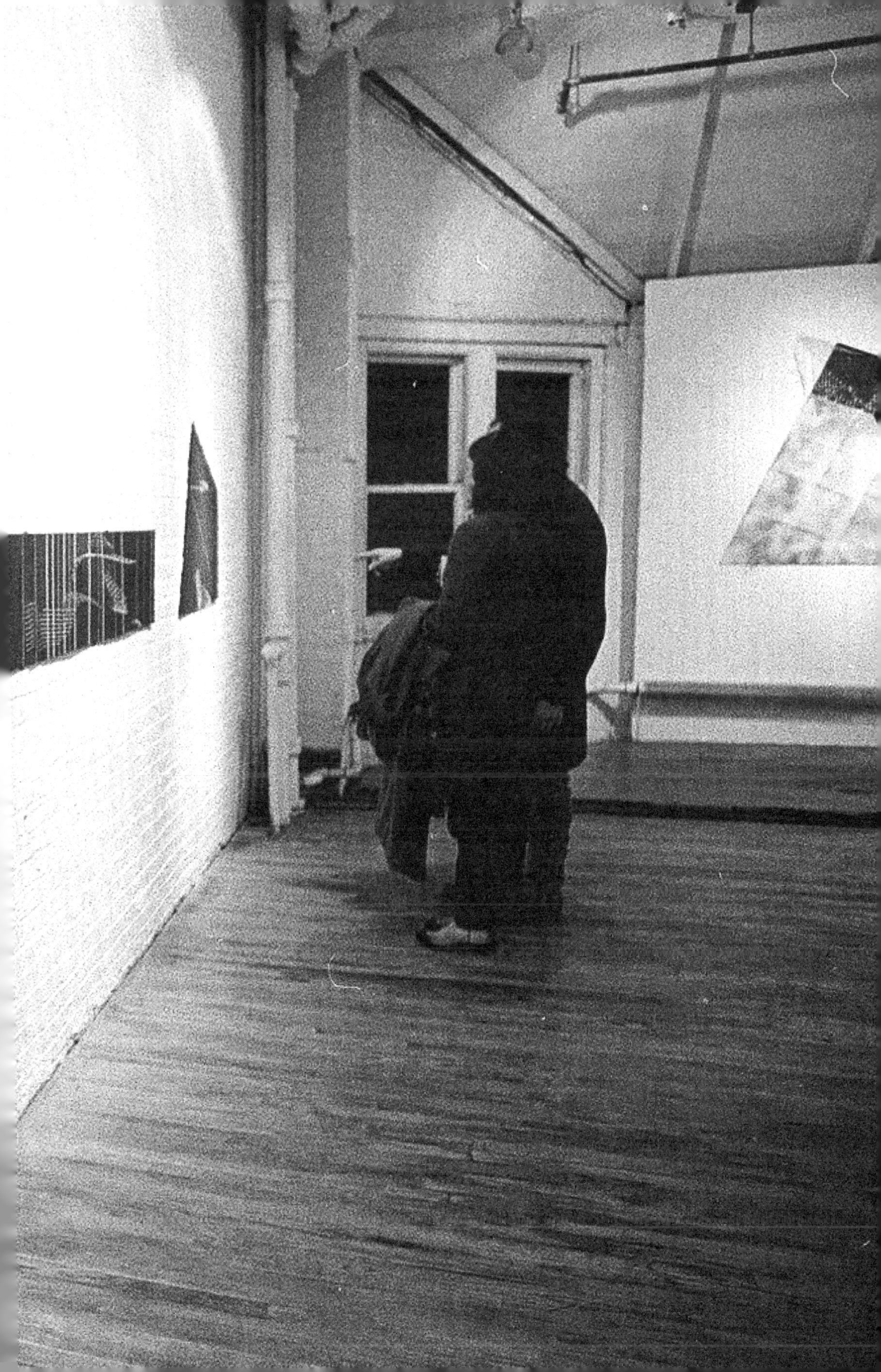

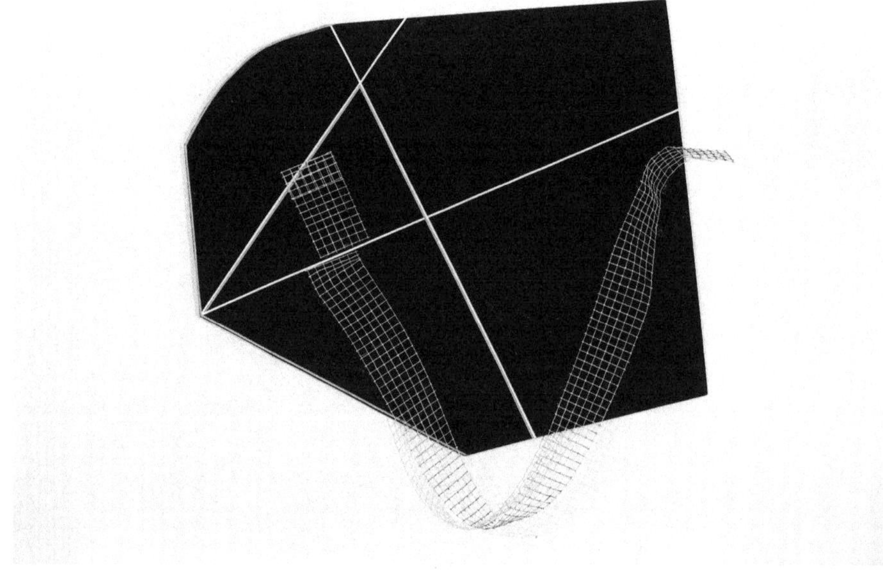

Untitled: Swing-Time, 1980–81
Mixed-media sculpture, dimensions unknown.

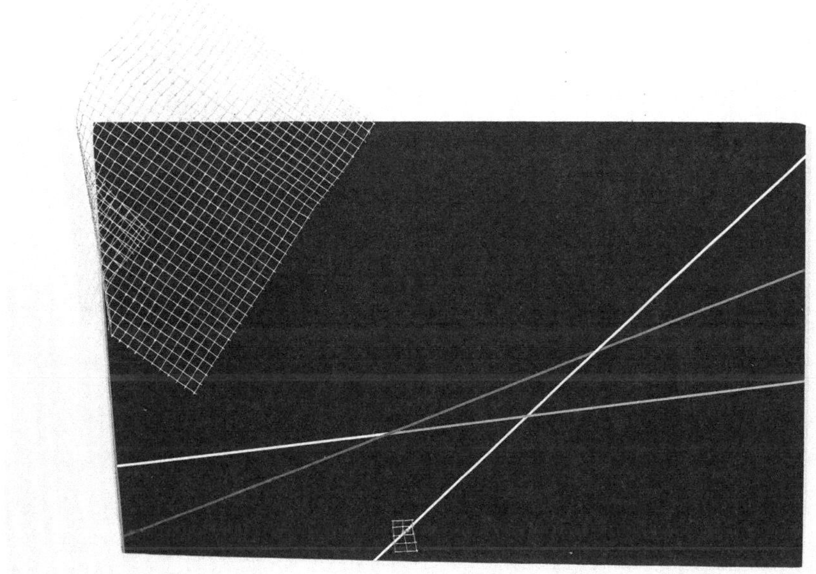

Paths, 1980–81
Mixed-media sculpture, 22 × 37 ½ × 22 ½ in.

Statement of Current Work

The work that I am doing has developed over the past two years. It had its beginnings in a visual image. In order to describe the image I carried it in my mind, I wrote a poem.

I see cosmic stalactites hanging
in the black of space

I see two and three dimensional
stalactites hanging in the dark of
space

I see them in a dark space
with little light shining upon
them

Shining upon their face, which face?

When the face can be seen from all sides,
when the hanging stalactite is as its
own earth and from without can be
seen from all sides at once by
many

* * *

This art particularly concerns time. Space, as in outer space (represented by the black). Space, as the occurrence of intervals. Intervals of space and time. Rather than the amount of time and what occurs in that interval, which is revealed as space and time, space as the area in which an event occurs.

How does this statement relate to the work, how does the viewer relate to the work?

1) The black represents the black of outer space. The vertical lines (as they appear in each piece, and where they appear in a piece) represent intervals of time, and the area, thereby, the space in which the event occurs. In addition, the verticals also serve as decorative function to the total ground which is black.

   There are additionally pieces where the diagonal is used. In these pieces the diagonal is used to represent out, or along what lines, time is traveling. For instance, if the diagonal is set at a 45 angle, then time is moving at the speed of light. If the diagonal is at an angle less than 45 then time is moving in a space like matter. This means that it is moving at earth time (our time movement is also space-like). If the angle is greater than 45 then time is moving greater than the speed of light. This use of the diagonal adds to the dimensions of each piece where they appear, and also serves a compositional function as well as decorative, and is intrinsic to each piece.

2) The mesh that appears on the surface of the black also serves as a twofold instrument - a) the mesh and its shadow also intensify the ground of the pieces. So, the ground relationship to the mesh has several aspects that solidify the ground. b) and most importantly, there are two pieces of mesh. The two pieces of mesh represent a rather difficult idea. That idea being the existence of a body without human contact, or rather before human contact (ex. You know that other countries exist without personal knowledge). Therefore, one piece of mesh (the smaller) represents a body in space, existing before any human consciousness has touched it. The larger piece of mesh represents the shape of the body as it is seen by a human being. The two bodies in each piece are changed or different from each other. This is because the interval of time between the unknowing existence of the body and the time the body has been sighted, the unknown body has changed. Those changes could be anything, from position to the reshaping of the body, by any particular cosmic occurrence. This larger piece is larger precisely because it is seen through a telescope, it makes the body appear larger ot the naked eye, while the smaller piece of mesh is smaller precisely because it is perceived as farther away.

3) How does the viewer relate to this type of work? My hope is that the viewer may see a relationship between the two pieces, but before that they should see the compositional relationships between all parts of each individual piece. The viewer should relate to the overall simplicity of each piece, as though it were a painting in three dimensions.

Concerning the significance of my involvement in this project:
The public is rarely given the opportunity to deal with art that is outside ordinary experience of nature and art though the art may be somewhat esoteric. Frankly, I know why this has been the case, but after a few exhibitions I am certain that the viewer is better off making his/her own judgment of what is understandable. I happen to believe that while art may be escapist in some respects it can also be intellectually stimulating in its sobriety-physically stimulating in its ardor of color and/or movement.

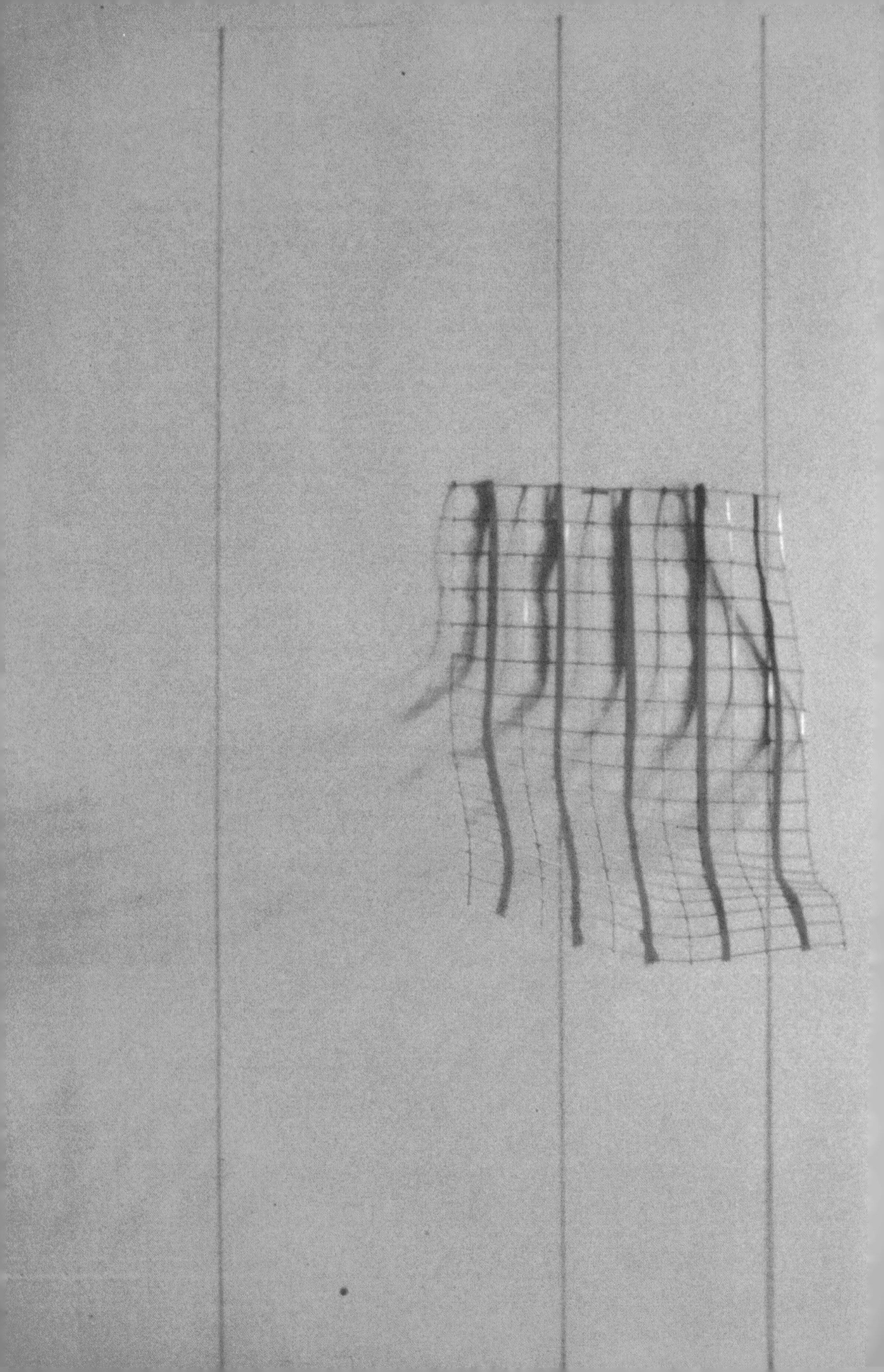

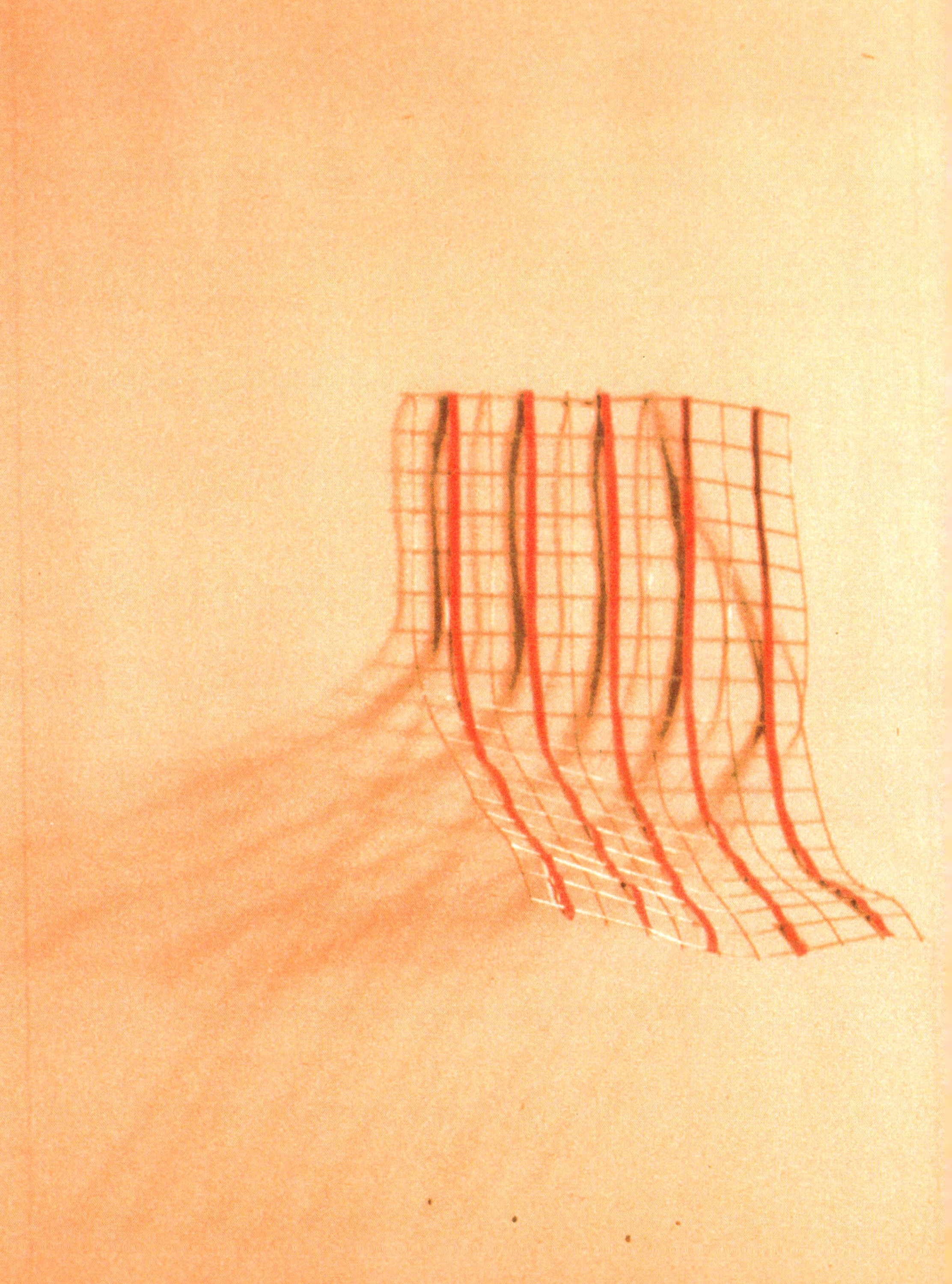

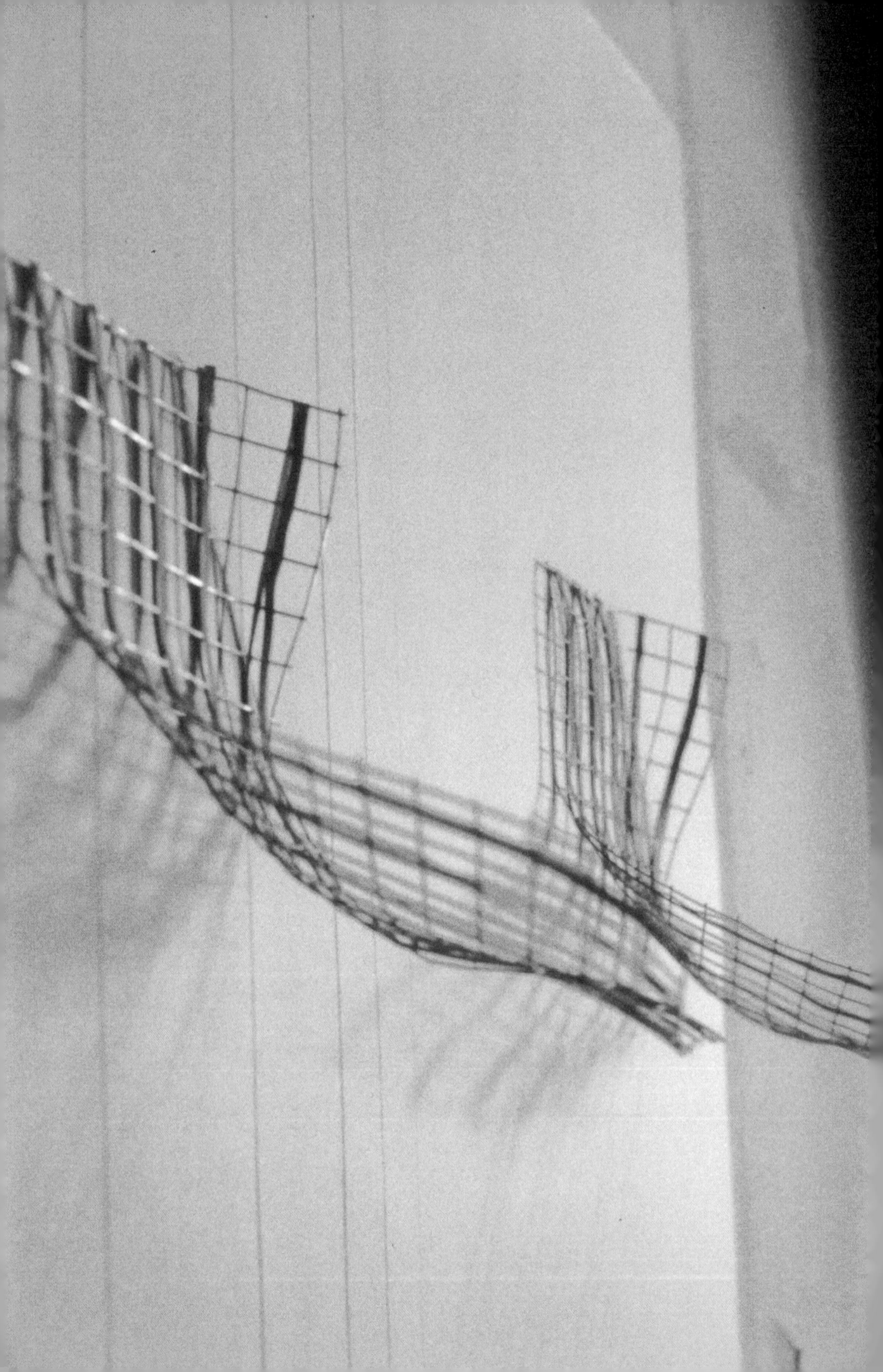

Facing, and previous spread:
Untitled, c. 1980
Wire mesh, red charting tape, dimensions unknown.

The last entry in this manuscript is dated November 25, 1980. The last few sentences of this entry imply that I am continuing to produce new pieces while complaining about the work and my own work ethic. I guess that was normal for me at the time. In spite of such frustrations, I kept making art and writing about my work and ideas.

Through 1981, I continued the sculptural series featured in this manuscript. The work made the following years, through 1984, included pastel drawings (Fig. 11) and paintings on paper (Fig. 12). I consider the content of that work to be an extension of the relief with wire pieces (see foreword, Fig. 9). The works on paper were followed by a set of three-dimensional, wall-mounted trapezoidal boxes (Fig. 13). This, in turn, gave way to a free-standing, life-size version, which I showed in a solo exhibition at the University of Miami and then donated to

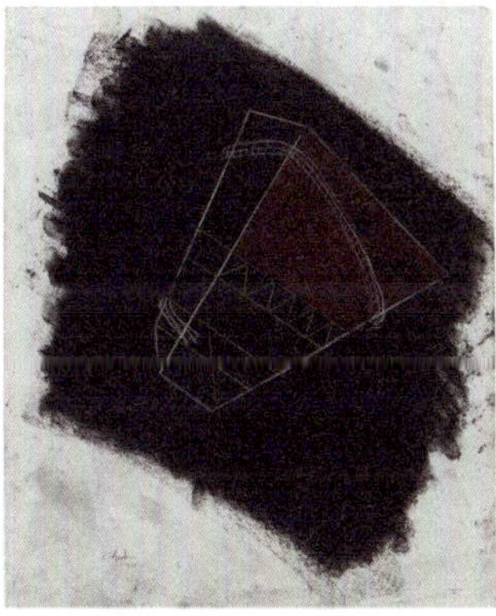

Fig. 11, *Untitled*, 1981. Charcoal and pastel on paper, 17 × 14 in.

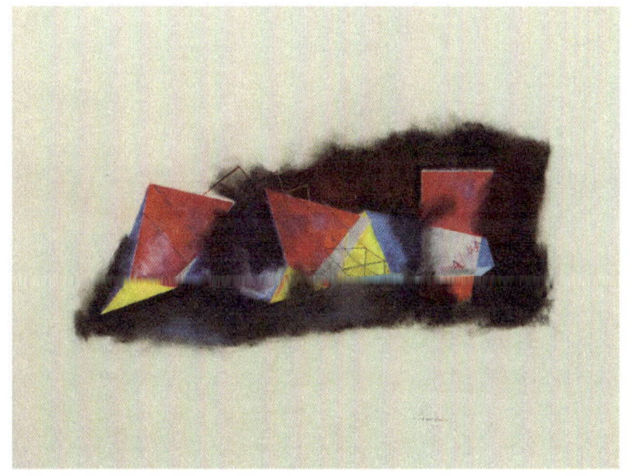

Fig. 12, *Untitled*, 1982. Charcoal and pastel on paper, 22¾ × 30 in.

the university gallery's collection (Fig. 14). By 1985, sculpture had run its course because I did not have a storage space. I remember the artist Terry Adkins—with whom I taught in the art department at SUNY New Paltz—saying that he only made sculpture when he had an exhibition for the same reason as I did: limited space.

From 1985 on, I continued my practice in painting. The mark-making begun back in the mid-1970s appeared on the trapezoid box sculptures and has reverberated through my work since. I combined techniques again, merging mark-making and expressionism. During 1986 I began a series I can only call an *Investigation into Green* (Fig. 15) and followed that work with

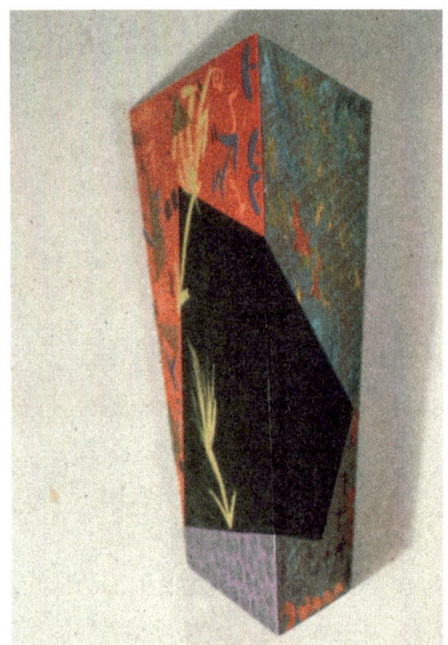

Fig. 13, *Places that Lay North of Here*, 1984. Acrylic on wood wall-hung trapezoidal box, 19 × 15 ½ × 7 ½ × 8 in.

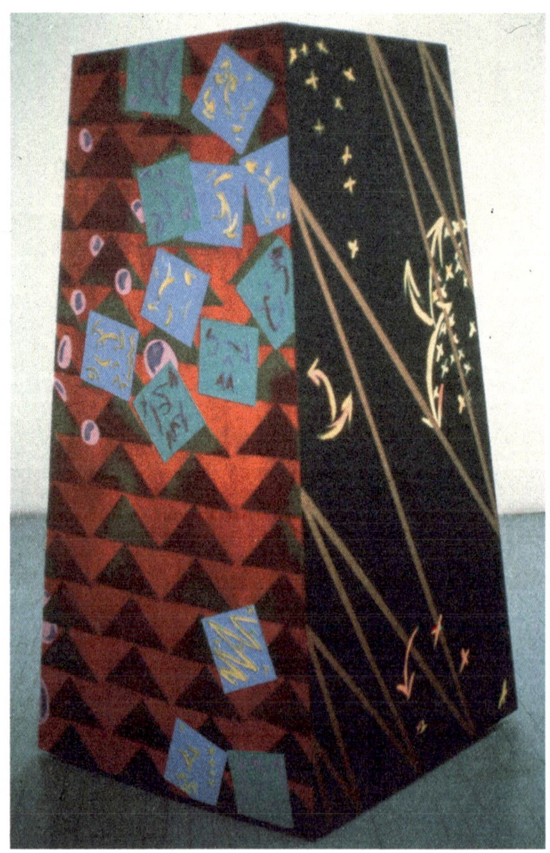

Fig. 14, *Northern Peeks, at Secrets There*, 1984. Acrylic on wood free-standing life-size box, 74 × 36 × 40 in.

several paintings incorporating vivid pinks and blues. These paintings have multiple layers through which marks and gestural brushwork can be seen. In 1988–89 I moved on from abstract expressionism; the last such painting, completed during my residency at the Studio Museum in Harlem, was *Plato's Cave* (Fig. 16).

By the late spring of 1989, I began to require more structure in my painting practice. For the second time, I read Susanne K. Langer's *Philosophy in a New Key: A Study in the Symbolism of Reason, Rite, and Art*. Of particular interest were her chapters "The Logic of Signs and Symbols" and "Discursive Forms and Presentational Forms." Informed by Langer's ideas, I made *The Currency of Meaning*, a series of about seventeen paintings in which I expanded my vocabulary of forms that approximated language. I also, again, combined expressionism with that language of ancient written forms, numbers, and geometric shapes (Fig. 17).

In 1988 I decided to pursue an MFA so I could teach painting at a college. I attended Maryland Institute College of Art. On arrival, I was still working on *The Currency of Meaning*, but by the following year I began a new series titled *The Creed of Athanasius and the Temple Curtain*. For my thesis exhibition in 1991, I made five large paintings, one of which was titled *The Calling* (Fig. 18). These works are founded in spirituality as I was then involved in the Episcopal Church.

Upon graduating and moving to Connecticut, I continued in this vein with a new series, *Psalms 100*, comprised of one hundred 17" × 18" paintings of circular shapes of variously monochromatic hues, which I worked on from 1992 to 1994. I considered Psalms to be an installation. I moved to Pennsylvania and began to consider natural forms and the natural environment more deeply, leading to the two series, *Natural Forms, Natural Things Part 1* and *Natural Things Part 2*, executed from 1995 to 1999 (Fig. 19).

After *Natural Things* I started looking upward and decided to read about astronomy and physics, especially black holes—exciting material to work with and reinvent. That study led to the series *Clusters: Stellar and Earthly*, 2003–2004 (Fig. 20), which spun off into several minor drawing series.

In 2007 came *Signs of Civilization*, a series built on sketches of land masses made from 30,000 feet (Fig. 21). After completing these works in 2011, I periodically produced prints and small paintings. I came to realize and accept that I did not like making small paintings; I realigned my space so I could work larger. The first large piece of any interest to me—a piece which has charged my enthusiasm for my practice—was *The Other Side of the Aquila Rift*, made in 2019 (Fig. 22). Since then, my practice has accelerated, and I am loving my work.

Overall, what is probably most important to note here is the continuity of my practice. My toolbox of forms and methods has continued to expand to include natural forms, both earthly and stellar; new uses of math, color, and spatial depth; new ways of applying paint; and new materials that allow the forms I use to manifest differently.

Fig. 15, *Investigation into Green (Green with Gold)*, 1986. Oil on canvas, 72 × 24 in.

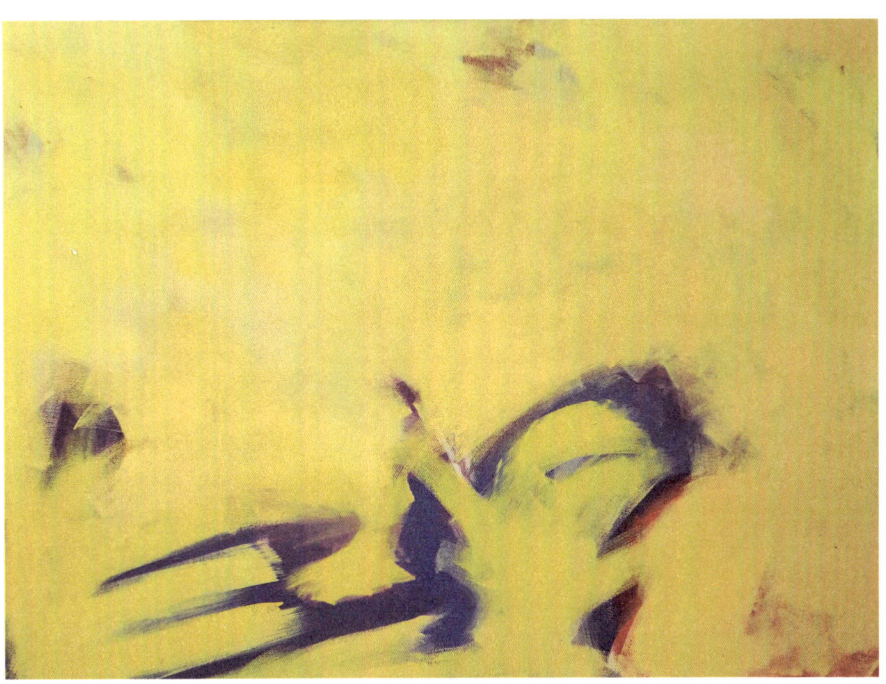

Fig. 16, *Plato's Cave*, 1988.
Oil on canvas, 56 × 76 in.

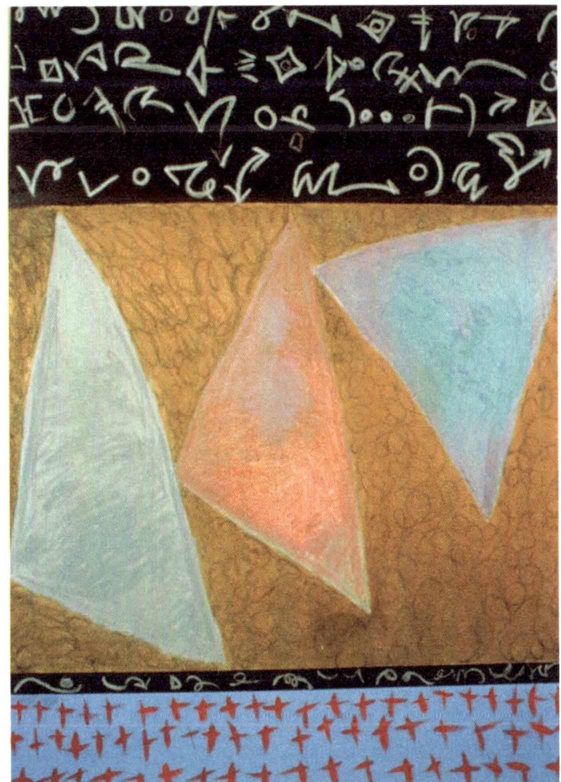

Fig. 17, *Currency of Meaning #16*, 1989. Oil on canvas, 68 × 50 in.

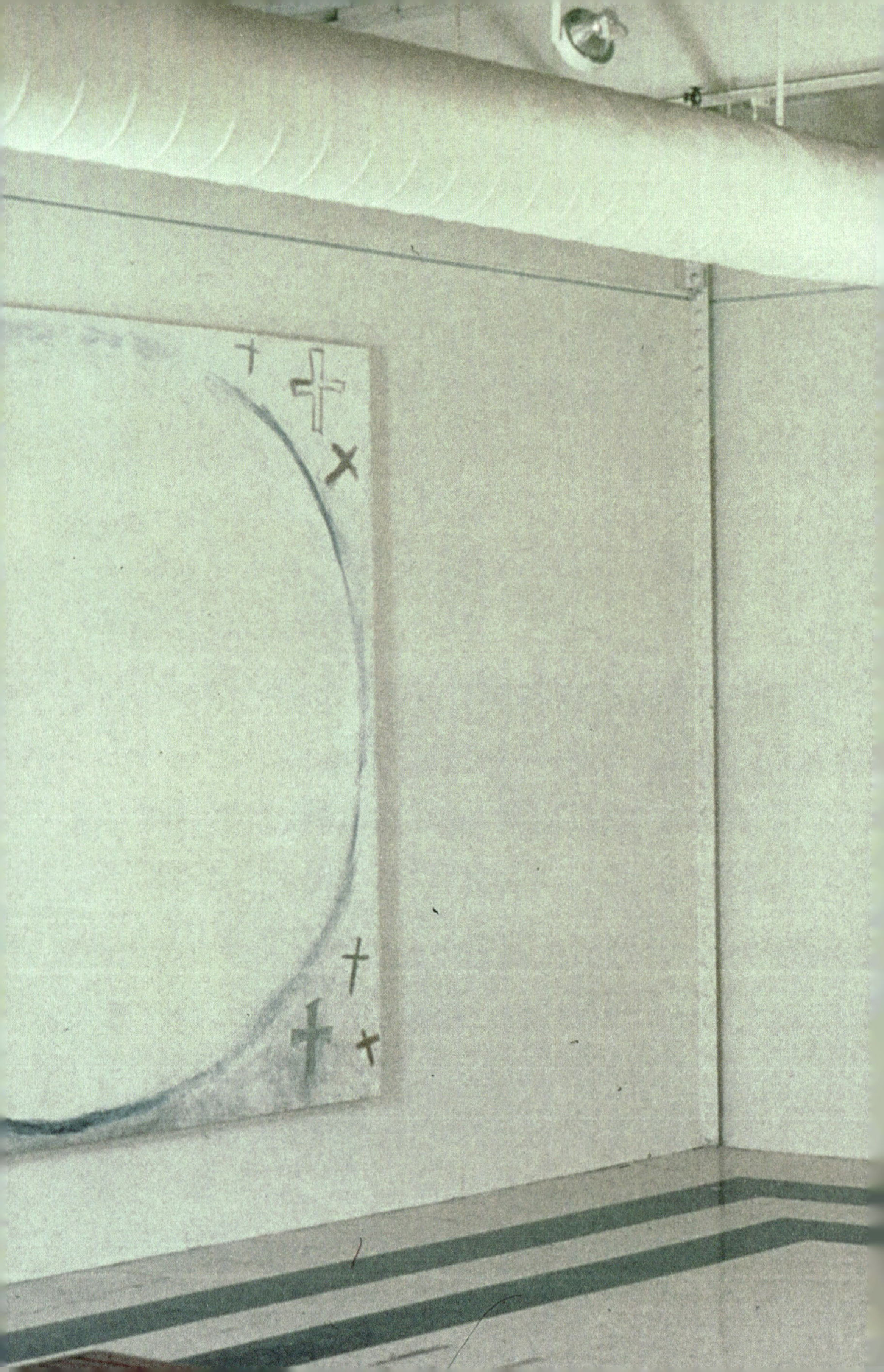

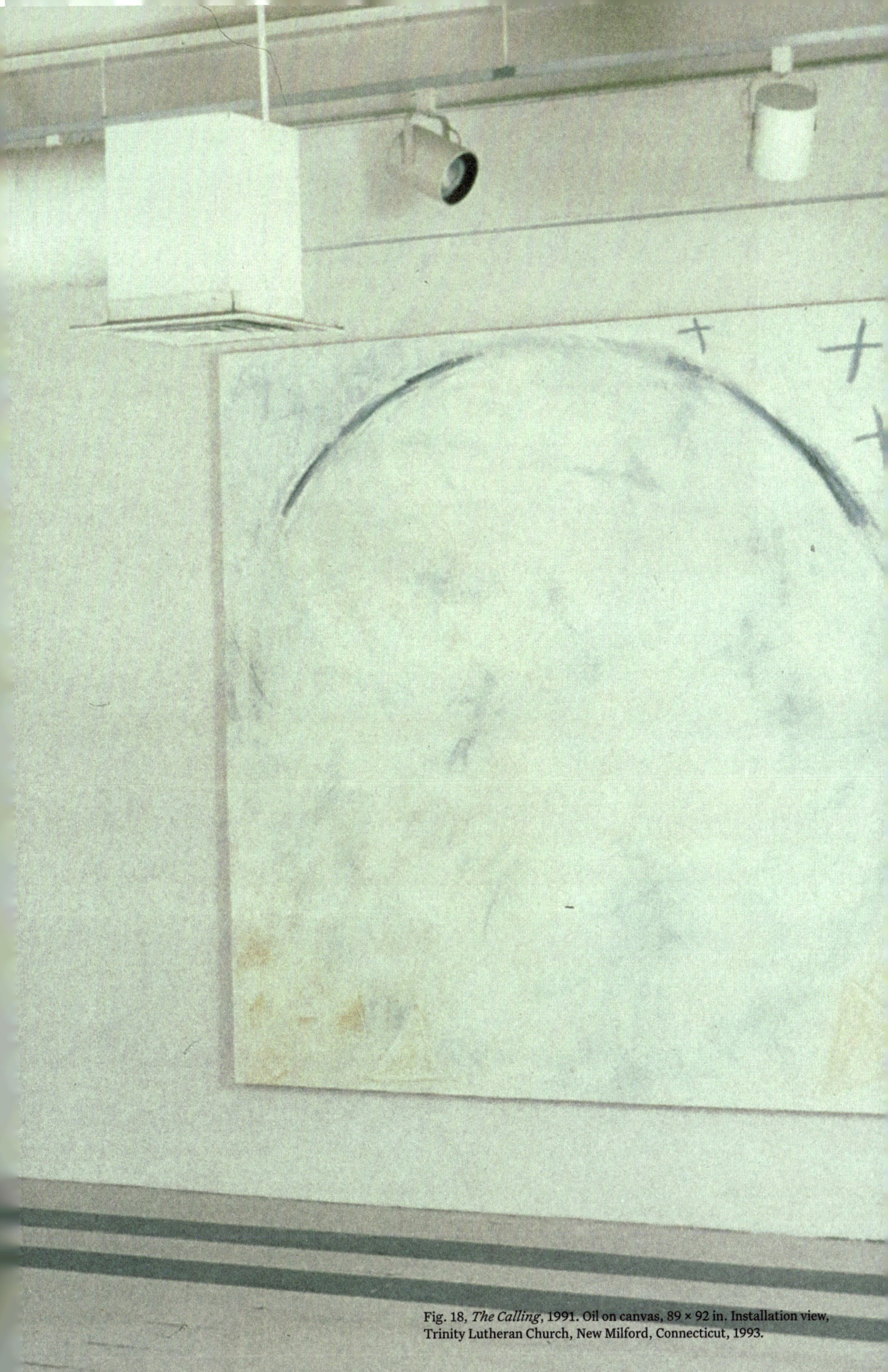

Fig. 18, *The Calling*, 1991. Oil on canvas, 89 × 92 in. Installation view, Trinity Lutheran Church, New Milford, Connecticut, 1993.

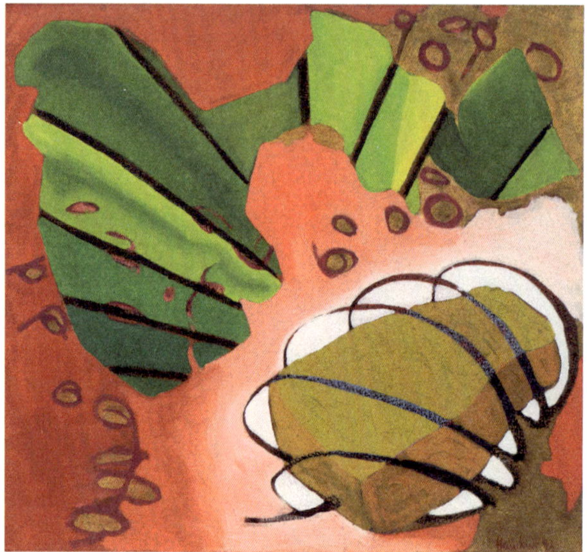

Fig. 19, *Natural Things #5*, 1996. Oil on canvas, 22 × 24 in.

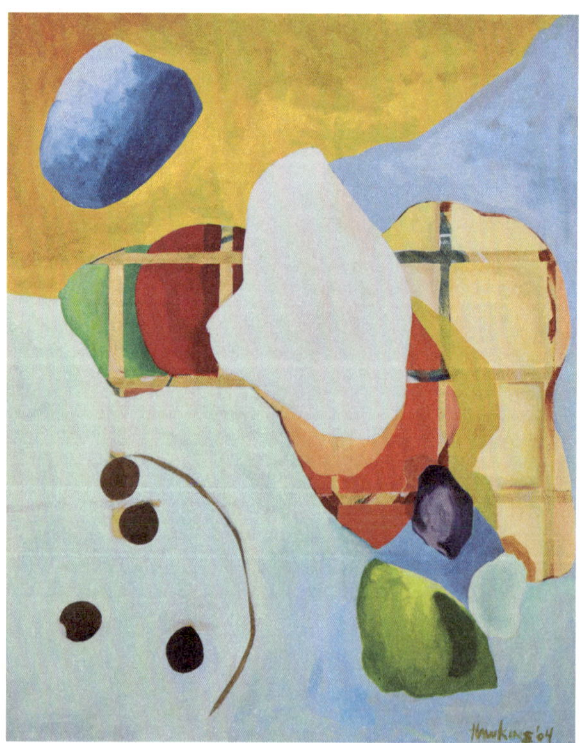

Fig. 20, *Clusters: Eta and Ecrux Don't Live in the Same Neighborhood*, 2004. Acrylic on canvas, 50 × 40 in.

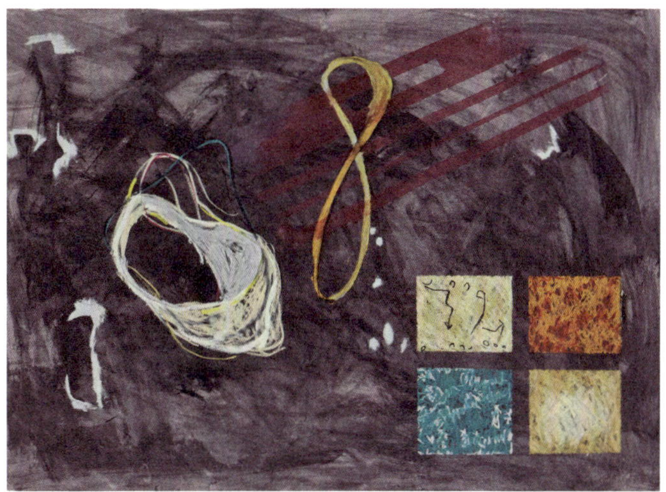

Fig. 21, *Signs of Civilization #5*, 2007–2010. Mixed media on paper, 29 x 41 in.

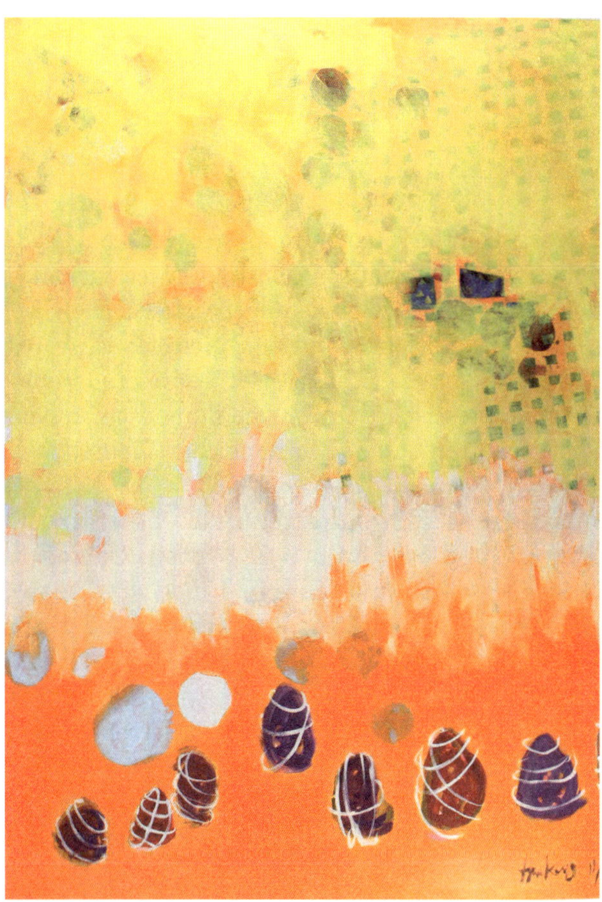

Fig. 22, *The Other Side of the Aquila Rift*, 2019. Acrylic on canvas, 76 × 56 in.

Art Notes, Art spent a long time in its binder waiting to be edited and published. I wrote it from 1979 to 1981, and since then, I've carried it around in various boxes and crates, always planning to publish it somehow. The document's time has arrived, and I want to thank those who helped bring it about.

Since this manuscript covers the preparatory events and work that preceded my solo exhibition at Just Above Midtown/Downtown in 1981—after the gallery's move from West 57th Street to Franklin Street in SoHo—I must first thank the extraordinary Linda Goode Bryant and her gallery partner in the early years, David Hammons, for allowing me to exhibit my work in the 1978 group show, *"It's a Crowd": Summer Group Exhibition*. This was my first professional exhibition beyond college.

I was a devotee of Just Above Midtown. I went to the gallery often—every weekend—just to be around Linda and those who worked with her, meeting the artists who would soon include my work in various group exhibitions in and around the New York City area. Thank you!

One such artist whom I enjoyed talking to was Janet Olivia Henry. Through David Hammons, I also met Corrine Jennings and Joe Overstreet, founders of Kenkeleba House (now Kenkeleba House Museum). Both JAM and Kenkeleba House were founded and led by African American artists. There I found my people, a community of artists spanning medium, race, and class, and I have not forgotten Linda's brother or her children.

Art Notes, Art is full of references to other artists whom I engaged with on practically a daily basis. One of those was Irene Wheeler, a ceramic sculptor I met at Queens College. Irene was older than me, but we became good friends right away. I miss her intelligent discourse about our work, and yes, driving the wrong way down streets to and from meetings with our artist group Ten Women. I thank Irene and the other members of Ten Women.

Today this manuscript could not have arrived in the flesh without its editor and my assistant, Ananth Shastri. I do have to thank my daughter Ianna for enthusiastically supporting this and every other project I partake in. It was

Ianna who recommended Ananth, and I am grateful for their very thorough work on this book project. It would not have happened without them.

For a book to see the light of day it needs a publisher and I have been privileged to work with Christopher Schwartz, gallerist at STARS gallery in Los Angeles. I am grateful for his support and exhibition of my work, and that, incredibly, he decided to support this manuscript by sending it to the Center for Art, Research and Alliances in New York. It is there that it was broadly welcomed. Ananth and I have had the great fortune to work with the extraordinary editor, Rachel Valinsky, and designer, Elizabeth Karp-Evans at Pacific. We all hope the book will provide some clarity about the early years of my practice working in a fraught period that witnessed social revolution on several fronts. Thank you.

Finally, I thank my friends who have been there through Covid and beyond: Victor Davson, Cicely Cottingham, Lawrence Philp, Celia Reisman, Susan Stedman, Petra Chu (who has supported my writing projects since we met), and my new friends Carter Cue and Julia Trotta. And my family—they have kept me on the straight and narrow. They have supported my work as an artist from the crib and beyond. Thank you Ianna, poet, scholar, and entrepreneur; thank you Zachary, writer and programmer; thanks to Sean and his family for their love, and to Richard and his family for theirs. And thank you to my sisters and brothers, my mother Elease, my father Robert. John Owen, thank you for being my partner through thick and thin—husband, photographer, and chef, oh, and carpenter.

Editor: Ananth Shastri
Managing Editor: Rachel Valinsky
Designer: Pacific (Elizabeth Karp-Evans and Adam Turnbull, with assistance from Ayline Le Sourd)
Copy Editor: Kaye Cain-Nielsen
Printer: die Keure Printing, Belgium
Image Retouching: Altaimage, New York

ISBN: 978-1-954939-05-9
LCCN: 2024939552

Image Credits:
All works/images courtesy of the artist unless otherwise noted. Every effort has been made to credit all images correctly.

pp. 7 (Fig. 1), 9 (Fig. 5), 173 (Figs. 11–12), 180–81 (Fig. 20–21) Photos: Timothy Doyon; pp. 9 (Fig. 6), 12–13, 158–59, 162–65 Photos: Steven Chaiken; p. 9 (Fig. 7) Courtesy of the artist and STARS, Los Angeles. Photo: Paul Salverson; p. 21 © Bernar Venet, ADAGP Paris, 2024. Courtesy of the artist; p. 42 Courtesy of Adrienne Wheeler; p. 69 Estate of David Smith, New York. © 2024 The Estate of David Smith / Licensed by VAGA at Artists Rights Society (ARS), NY; p. 70 Courtesy of Hirschl & Adler Modern, New York, and the Estate of Louisa Chase. Photo: Eric W. Baumgartner; p. 78 © Howardena Pindell. Photo: Digital Image © The Museum of Modern Art/Licensed by SCALA / Art Resource, NY; p. 84 Courtesy of The Clinton Hill Estate. Photo: Cameron Crone; p. 123 Private collection. © APRA Foundation Berlin; p. 126 Both images © Vivian Browne; Courtesy of Adobe Krow Archives, Los Angeles, and RYAN LEE Gallery, New York; p. 127 Courtesy of Janet Olivia Henry; pp. 140–41 Courtesy of the Sandra M. Payne Trust and Barrett Barrera Projects. Photo: Andrea Callard; pp. 160–61 Photo: unknown; p. 176 (Fig. 15) Courtesy of the artist and Paula Cooper Gallery, New York. Photo: Timothy Doyon; p. 177 (Fig. 16) Collection: Kenkeleba House Museum, New York (Fig. 17) Private Collection. Photo: John Owen; pp. 178–79 Collection: Trinity Lutheran Church, New Milford, Connecticut. Photo: John Owen; pp. 180–81 (Fig. 19) Collection: Carla Chammas and Judi Roman. Photo: Paul Salveson (Fig. 22) Collection: Jennifer Stewart.

CARA would like to thank Paula Cooper Gallery, New York; kaufmann repetto, Milan/New York; and Hollybush Gardens, London, for their support of this publication.

Special thanks to Julia Trotta; Alexis Johnson, Paula Cooper Gallery; Francesca Kaufmann and Chiara Repetto, kaufmann repetto; Malin Ståhl, Hollybush Gardens; Christopher Schwartz, STARS; Julie Trotta; Bernar Venet Studio; Luke Smith-Stevens, The Estate of David Smith; Shelley Farmer, Hirschl & Adler Modern; Julian Corbett, Garth Greenan; Art Resource; Rick Royale, Royale Projects; Tiffany Phelon, Clinton Hill Estate; Adrian Piper Research Archive Foundation Berlin; Janet Olivia Henry; Andrea Callard; Bridget Melloy; projects+gallery; Ethel Renia, Ryan Lee Gallery; Susan Stedman; Adrienne Wheeler; and Lilia Taboada, The Museum of Modern Art, New York.

Distributed worldwide by
ARTBOOK | D.A.P.
75 Broad Street, Suite 630
New York, NY 10004
orders@dapinc.com
www.artbook.com

Center for Art, Research and Alliances (CARA)
225 West 13th Street
New York, NY 10011
www.cara-nyc.org

Center for Art,
Research and Alliances